57-7

PROBLEMS OF THE MODERN ECONOMY

The Goal of Economic Growth

PROBLEMS OF THE MODERN ECONOMY

General Editor: EDMUND S. PHELPS, *Yale University*

Each volume in this series presents
prominent positions in the debate of
an important issue of economic policy

The Goal of
Economic Growth

SOURCES · COSTS · BENEFITS

Edited with an introduction by

EDMUND S. PHELPS

YALE UNIVERSITY

NEW YORK

W · W · NORTON & COMPANY · INC ·

America Must Grow, by Walter Lippmann and Francis M. Bator. Abridged from *The Saturday Evening Post* (November 5, 1960). Copyright 1960 by The Curtis Publishing Company. Reprinted by permission of the authors.

Projections of Federal, State and Local Government Expenditures in 1967 (Table) from *The Challenge to America: Its Economic and Social Aspects* by Rockefeller Brothers Fund, Inc. Copyright 1958 by Rockefeller Brothers Fund, Inc. Reprinted by permission of Doubleday & Company, Inc.

Economic Growth as a National Goal, originally published as "High Employment and Growth in the American Economy," by Herbert Stein and Edward F. Denison, from the Report of the President's Commission on National Goals in *Goals for Americans* by The American Assembly, Columbia University, copyright 1960. Reprinted by permission of Prentice-Hall, Inc.

Public Responsibility for Growth and Stability (final paragraph) from *Economics: An Introductory Analysis* by Paul A. Samuelson. Copyright 1961 by McGraw-Hill Book Company, Inc. Used by permission.

Comparisons of United States and USSR National Output: Some Rules of the Game, by Abraham S. Becker. From *World Politics* (October 1960). Reprinted by permission of the author and The RAND Corporation.

Economic Growth: The Last Hundred Years, by Deborah C. Paige, with F. T. Blackaby and S. Freund. From the *National Institute Economic Review* (July 1961). Reprinted by permission of the National Institute of Economic and Social Research, 2 Dean Trench Street, London, S.W.1.

Growth Through Taxation, by James Tobin. From *The New Republic* (July 25, 1960). Reprinted by permission of *The New Republic*.

Tangible Investment as an Instrument of Growth, adapted from "The New View of Investment" by Edmund S. Phelps in *Quarterly Journal of Economics* (November 1962). Copyright 1962 by the President and Fellows of Harvard College. Reprinted by permission of the Harvard University Press.

Investment in Human Capital, by Theodore W. Schultz. From the *American Economic Review* (March 1961). Reprinted by permission of the author and the American Economic Association.

Underinvestment in College Education? by Gary S. Becker. From the *American Economic Review* (May 1960). Reprinted by permission of the author and the American Economic Association.

Research and Economic Growth: The Role of Public Policy, by Benton F. Massell and Richard R. Nelson. From the *California Management Review* (Winter 1962). Reprinted by permission of the *California Management Review*.

Can There Be Too Much Research? by Fritz Machlup. From *Science* (November 28, 1958). Reprinted by permission of the author and *Science*.

Acknowledgments

In the preparation of this volume I have benefited from the criticism and suggestions of many colleagues and students to whom I am grateful. I would like also to thank Robert Harlow for helping to prepare the list of further readings, and Mrs. Merle E. Hochman and Mrs. Sally S. Harrison for their assistance in preparing the book for publication. To Charlotte D. Phelps I owe a special debt of gratitude for manifold contributions to the preparation of the manuscript and the correction of proof.

E.S.P.

Contents

TABLE 1. *The Growth of Productive Capacity in the United States Economy 1900–1962.*

Total Annual Capacity Output in Selected Years
(1962 prices, in billions of dollars)

1900	1929	1947	1952	1957	1962
81	216	341	417	501	600

Annual Rates of Growth of Total Capacity Output
(In percent)

Terminal Year	Initial Year				
	1900	1929	1947	1952	1957
1929	3.5				
1947	3.1	2.6			
1952	3.2	2.9	4.1		
1957	3.3	3.0	3.9	3.7	
1962	3.3	3.1	3.8	3.7	3.7

Notes.—The growth rates are compounded annual rates of change of Total Capacity Output. Capacity Output—sometimes called Potential GNP —is the Gross National Product (in 1962 prices) obtainable through full utilization of the economy's existing resources. GNP is the market value of all final goods and services produced. For purposes of calculation, full utilization is defined as a 97% employment rate.

In estimating the level of GNP that an employment rate of 97% would have produced, it was assumed that a decline of the unemployment rate by one percentage point would raise actual GNP as a percentage of potential GNP by 3 points (in the postwar years and 2 points in the two prewar years).

Actual GNP data (in 1954 prices) are those of the U. S. Department of Commerce, with the exception of GNP in 1900, which is from the Kendrick-Kuznets series published in John W. Kendrick, *Productivity Trends in the United States* (Princeton, 1961). This series (in 1929 prices), which matches the Commerce estimate for 1929, was converted from 1929 to 1954 prices by means of the Commerce GNP deflator. The 1954 dollar series was converted to 1962 prices using the Commerce deflator which was estimated at 117.7 in mid-1962. Unemployment rates (adjusted to present-day definitions) are from the U. S. Department of Labor, with the exception of 1900, which is from the series of Stanley Lebergott in *The Measurement and the Behavior of Unemployment* (Princeton, 1957).

Introduction

THE ECONOMIC growth of this country was, until very recently, a matter of little popular interest. There was continual concern over the growth of *market demand* in relation to the growth of productive capacity: inflation was feared if demand grew too rapidly, unemployment was feared if demand grew too slowly. But the growth of *productive capacity* itself was not a source of worry. The nation's capacity to produce grew steadily decade after decade. The adequacy of the rate of growth, which had made this nation the most prosperous in the world, was not questioned.

The lack of popular concern over growth was reflected in government policy. We had no public policy toward the rate of growth. Many government activities, especially investments in the public sector, made a vital contribution to growth. Yet no branch of government ever took measures explicitly to alter the growth of the private economy where the great bulk of the goods and services are produced. Our public policies sought mainly to make the private economy efficient, equitable, and stable. Clearly an economy can achieve all these goals and yet not grow; pursuit of these goals did not necessarily stimulate growth. If the legislation, expenditures, taxes, and monetary operations by which government pursued these goals sometimes affected the rate of growth, this effect was typically a by-product. Government policies expressly designed to alter the growth of the private economy were not contemplated.

Now attitudes and public policy give signs of changing. After a brief postwar spurt ending about 1952, capacity has grown at an average annual rate of 3.7 percent. This is a respectable rate by our historical standards: it exceeds slightly our growth rate between 1900 and 1929, and it is far better than the dismal years of the Great Depression and World War II. But many people are no longer content with our average peacetime growth rate. They are calling growth a public responsibility. Government measures to raise the rate of growth are being proposed. President Kennedy has declared 4½ percent annual growth in this decade as a goal of public policy.

Yet the idea of accelerating our economic growth has, quite properly, raised many questions and controversies. Do we, the richest nation in the world, need to be richer? What benefits could faster growth confer that we cannot have now through better use of our existing resources? Is the control of our growth a proper function of government? Can government avoid affecting the rate of growth? These questions are taken up in Part One of this volume.

Part Two considers the prospects for growth. In view of past trends here and abroad, how fast can we hope to grow over the next decade? How large is the Soviet economy relative to ours? Is Russia likely to catch up?

Finally, what are the means of economic growth? Which are best? Part Three examines what economists have learned about how to grow and what is being done to implement this knowledge.

GROWTH: A NEW GOAL OF PUBLIC POLICY?

The first essay, by Walter Lippmann and Francis Bator, argues that faster growth is a necessity if, first, we are to meet rapidly increasing public needs—needs like national defense which seem to increase faster than our national income—and if, second, we are to enjoy an adequately rising private standard of living. Unless we raise our rate of growth, they state, "we shall have to choose between failure to meet the Soviet challenge—which would be intolerable—or we shall have to accept a much bleaker, much less open and hopeful way of life in America."

What growth rate would be adequate? Working from the 1959 level of the Gross National Product, Lippmann and Bator figure that a growth rate of 4 percent would be sufficient.[1] This growth program would enable us to reach the 1967 target levels of public expenditures proposed several years ago by the Rockefeller Fund and at the same time to allow private consumer expenditures to rise, but not as rapidly as in the 1950's.

Since this growth program was proposed, 1967 has drawn closer. Has our capacity to produce been growing at 4 percent in the 1960's so far? Not according to the estimates in Table 1.

1. Gross National Product, or GNP, is the market value of all goods and services produced in the economy.

To reach the Rockefeller targets, capacity will probably need to grow faster than 4 percent in the years remaining.

Whatever the appropriate rate of growth, how can we realize it? Lippmann and Bator suggest we can promote growth through government action. They propose that the government in making its decisions about taxes, spending, tariffs, interest rates, and so forth, should take into account the effect of these decisions on growth and so exploit its power for stimulating growth.

Herbert Stein and Edward Denison question much of this thesis. They believe that the need for faster growth has not always been well reasoned. If we are going without public services which are needed *now,* then the most rational response would seem to be simply to supply them. Should inflation threaten, we can cut back less badly needed public or private expenditures. It ought to be the least needed goods and services for which we must wait until the capacity of our economy is able to meet them.

To validate the unmet-social-needs argument, Stein and Denison suggest, it must be assumed that we are the victims of a system which has "locked" government expenditure at some fixed proportion of national income. If we cannot change the share of resources committed to the public sector, then we shall have to make GNP grow exactly as fast as we want the public sector to grow.

Alas, insofar as the things which governments purchase rise *in price* in proportion to per capita real national income, this desperate method of satisfying public needs at a faster rate will not work. Raising the productivity of the private sector will also raise the real wages of the engineers, teachers, lawyers, and professional soldiers that the public sector wants to employ. Unless the productivity of people in government employment rises too (and productivity trends have been slower there), the public sector will need to spend more just to maintain a constant amount of employment and to get a constant amount of work done. So we may have to face up after all to a rise of government spending as a share of national income if we want to satisfy significantly more public needs than we have been doing.

Yet growth facilitates a change in the share of national resources allocated to the satisfaction of unmet public needs. Could we afford present government programs without our past growth? By raising the productivity of private industry we can meet the demand for private goods in our economy with fewer workers.

Rising productivity in the private sector will release resources for public use *with no loss of private output*. Similarly, if we could find a way to raise the productivity of the public sector—and automation is beginning to play a role in both military and civilian agencies—resources there would be released for use in the private sector or in new uses in the public sector. *In any case, the growth of productivity expands the opportunities of the economy.*

Stein and Denison touch on another issue which is raised in the Lippmann-Bator essay. They call it a "real and serious issue" whether the government should take deliberate steps to alter the national rate of growth. They cite the "alternative view" that the "desirable rate of growth and the correct means to achieve it are those that would emerge from private decisions." Just such a view seems to be taken by W. Allen Wallis.

Wallis feels, first of all, that many proposals to accelerate economic growth threaten individual freedom. The "modern mercantilists" wish to "force" growth on the economy. Their approach involves compelling people to consume less either through taxes or through inflation, in order to free resources for investment and other growth-producing uses. He opposes "depressed" levels of consumption except in "dire emergency," and he sees none now. In view of this country's substantial lead over the Soviet Union and the rate at which we are already satisfying public needs, Wallis wishes to let growth emerge as the natural by-product of an economy in which the government's task is to strengthen equality of opportunity, individual initiative, and economic stability and to provide public services with "realism and restraint."

Wallis concludes that the "right" rate of growth in a free and efficient economy is "that rate which conforms to the voluntary choices of the people" rather than a rate obtained by "coercion."

Paul Samuelson's essay relates to this issue. He contends first that the government *can* control the level of investment in the economy—private investment as well as public investment—by the way it chooses among various monetary and fiscal instruments in its efforts to control the level of employment in the economy. For example, a "tight" money policy and a compensating "easy" fiscal policy boosts consumption, reduces investment, and hence reduces the rate of growth. He believes the range of choice among these policy instruments is sufficiently wide that we can have whatever level of employment *and* rate of growth that our society wishes to have.

Samuelson also points out that every modern economy necessarily follows certain monetary and fiscal policies. Every society *must choose* how to use its policy instruments. Therefore, the government *does* control investment and growth and cannot avoid doing so.

Samuelson's view has important implications for Wallis' position. If it is true that the government is confronted with such choices, then is the present rate of growth necessarily the "right" one? Personal consumption expenditures are typically made in a voluntary manner; but if the *level* of voluntary consumption is partly the product of government decisions about taxes and so forth, can we be sure we happen to have the right level? The principle of voluntarism appears to validate any aggregate consumption level, whence any rate of aggregate investment and growth.

Stein and Denison recognize that "the rate of growth emerging from private decisions is inevitably affected by the action of the government in discharging its important functions." Yet they question, without committing themselves, whether these functions should be extended to include "the explicit determination" of the rate of growth. But what if Samuelson is right that the government must choose among more than one way to discharge important functions like maintaining high employment: then how can the government (and the people who elect it) escape responsibility for the effect of its decisions on the rate of growth? Should the government, ostrich-like, make its decisions in ignorance or in disregard of their consequences for growth? [2]

2. The reader may want to ponder the following question: Could the government follow a deliberately "neutral" policy toward growth? That is, could the government be guided in its tax and monetary decisions by preferences revealed in the marketplace? Lippmann and Bator assert that "the government cannot be neutral even if it wants to be." They may have in mind the fact that the government alone must make the vital decisions about public expenditures. These public goods are an important constituent of economic welfare and the increase in their supply an important element in "growth." However, once these expenditures are decided upon, would it not be possible to finance them so as to distort as little as possible the individual decisions affecting the growth of the private economy? But then the ques-

In any case, no government in this country can any longer be unaware of or unconcerned about the enormous impact of its decisions on the rate of growth of the economy. The real questions about growth are centering now over what rate of growth to aim at and over the most effective means to realize that growth rate. As all the writers in this volume recognize, one of the most important considerations in this regard is the growth of the Soviet Union. The larger the Russian economy, the greater is the military and economic offensive that it can mount.

OUTLOOK FOR THE "ECONOMIC RACE"

How fast is the Soviet economy growing? How large has it become? As Wallis indicates, these questions have no simple answers. When we add up the Russians' heterogeneous product mix and compare it to the menu of goods produced here, we have to put *price tags* on the corn, caviar, machine tools, and missiles which we and they produce. But whose price tags, theirs or ours? It makes a big difference; machine tools are cheap relative to corn in the USSR in comparison to their prices in the United States.

Abraham Becker reports that if we evaluate Russian and American outputs at American prices—and these are the ones we are familiar with—then Soviet GNP was about two thirds of our GNP in 1958. Even if Russia's growth rate should fall to 6 percent and we manage a growth rate of 4 percent, the Soviet GNP will reach three quarters of the U. S. GNP by 1965.

Quite apart from the cold war, it is intriguing to speculate whether Russia can catch the United States economically as Great Britain once went ahead of France and as this country overtook Britain. The economic "lead" has changed hands before and it may do so again.

Table 2 shows the implications of growth rates for the "economic race." The United States growth rates in the top row and the Soviet growth rates in the left-hand column signify average annual rates of increase of these countries' GNP. Note that every

---

tion is, are these private decisions also in the interest of the nation? What if private citizens are not correctly informed of desirable future public expenditure programs and the ways they are to be financed? What if social and private returns to investment and saving differ? For these reasons a neutral or market-guided public policy toward growth is not likely to be optimal.

item in both the Russian and American GNP is valued at its 1960 American price. The table assumes that in 1960 the Soviet GNP (in terms of our prices) was still only two thirds of ours. (This is plausible because of special factors which favored United States growth and reduced Soviet growth between 1958 and 1960.)

Suppose the Soviet Union maintains its average postwar growth rate of 7 percent and we move along at 3 percent. Then, as one can read from the table, Soviet GNP (measured in the way indicated) will exceed ours sometime in 1970.

TABLE 2. *Date of Russian "Lead" in the U.S.-USSR Economic Race*

USSR Growth Rate	United States Growth Rate		
	3%	4%	5%
5%	1980	2001	——
6%	1974	1980	2001
7%	1970	1974	1980
8%	1968	1970	1974

Or suppose the Russian economy slows down to 6 percent and we manage a 5 percent growth rate. Then we will stay ahead until 2001.[3] By this time relative GNP's may matter very little to us. Observe that the year at which the economic "lead" changes hands depends only on the *difference* between the two growth rates.

How fast do the Russians aim to grow? And how fast can we reasonably hope to grow during the 1960's? Khrushchev forecasts a better than 10 percent increase in "national income" (Soviet definition) in the 1960's, with some slow-down in the next decade. His stated goals for 1980 imply an 8 percent rate of growth over the entire twenty-year program. (However, the Soviet-defined national income gives less weight to the more slowly growing services than does the Western version of national income.)

The President's Council of Economic Advisers looks forward

3. Such simple GNP comparisons require several qualifications: the difference between Gross and Net Product, the difference in population and therefore consumption per capita, the artificiality of evaluating, say, 1980 GNP's at 1960 prices, the possibly different efficiencies of the countries in satisfying consumer preferences, and many others.

to a 4.9 percent rate of increase of Real GNP in the 1960's in this country. This is predicated on the growth of capacity at a 4.3 percent rate and on an improvement in the utilization of capacity. But neither can be taken for granted. If we do no better with our unemployment problem in the middle and late 1960's than we did in the early years of this decade, capacity seems unlikely (to this observer) to grow faster than 4 percent.

These forecasts make one curious about past standards of growth. Has this country ever grown for a decade at better than 4 percent? Has productivity ever risen at 2.5 percent on average? In short, what is "par" in long-term growth rates?

The article by Deborah Paige and colleagues at the National Institute of Economic and Social Research in London is a fascinating study of the economic growth of eleven advanced countries over the past hundred years. The National Institute study shows that other Western democratic countries have exhibited growth rates above 5 percent for as long as a decade. Germany, Italy, and Japan have performed brilliantly since World War II. Sweden and Japan have for several decades been growing faster than we. But once, in the years before World War I, this country also grew quite rapidly. Can the United States repeat its pre-1913 growth rate?

Our rate of growth depends on how we use our inputs. Like consumer demands, public needs, or any economic want, the goal of long-term growth requires the expenditure of scarce resources. What are the principal means of growth? Which instruments of growth are the most effective, which the "best buy"?

THREE WAYS TO GROW

James Tobin suggests that we can increase our future capacity in three principal ways: we can devote our resources to increasing our stock of *capital goods;* we can employ resources in *research;* and we can allocate resources to the *education* of the population. Alternatively, if we would rather not grow, we can let our resources lie idle—unemployment frequently makes a large claim on our resources—or we can use them to provide the consumer goods and leisure which constitute a country's standard of living.

In making such growth-producing expenditures, we are giving up potential (if not actual) consumption. It would be correct to say therefore that all three means of growth constitute forms of investment. The effectiveness of these three kinds of investment in increasing our productive capacity, the manner in which they contribute to growth, are the concern of Part Three.

Tobin attaches great importance to investment in tangible capital. Since the early 1950's, annual private expenditures for plant and equipment have increased very little; private fixed investment has been dipping below 10 percent of GNP. This could provide part of the explanation for the detectable retardation of the economy since 1952.

How effective would increased investment be? Tobin suggests that an increase of fixed investment from 10 to 13 percent of GNP would raise the rate of growth some two percentage points— from about 3 percent per annum to about 5 percent.[4]

Many economists would question Tobin's approach. Economics teaches that each successive one-dollar increase in capital, or any other input, normally results in successively smaller increases in output. But Tobin—who has heard of this famous *law of diminishing returns*—is voicing the heresy that each dollar increase in capital will produce the same increase in output. Which view is correct?

In the next essay the editor provides a brief review of the prominent ideas of economists since the war about this relation between output and capital—or between the growth of output and the rate of investment. There is the idea used by Tobin of a fixed ratio of capital to output; as we saw, this notion seems "optimistic" as to the effectiveness of investment. And there is the classical idea, in various guises, of diminishing returns to capital; the classical notion is quite "pessimistic." Studies from this classi-

4. How was this calculation made? Tobin evidently starts with the formula: $\frac{\Delta O}{O} = \frac{\Delta O}{\Delta K} \times \frac{\Delta K}{O}$,

where O is output (GNP), K is capital, and where ΔO and ΔK denote the annual change in output and capital respectively. $\Delta O/O$ is the rate of growth and ΔK is investment net of replacement (depreciation).

Tobin assumes that every \$1 increase in O requires an increase in K of \$1.50. Therefore $\frac{\Delta O}{\Delta K} = \frac{2}{3}$. Tobin estimates gross investment at about 10 percent of output, and net investment at about 5 percent of output. Hence $\frac{\Delta K}{O} = \frac{5}{100}$. So $\frac{\Delta O}{O} = \frac{\Delta O}{\Delta K} \times \frac{\Delta K}{O} = \frac{2}{3} \times \frac{5}{100} = \frac{10}{300} = 3\frac{1}{3}$. If gross investment were increased to 13% of output, net investment would rise to 8% of output. Then $\frac{\Delta O}{O} = \frac{2}{3} \times \frac{8}{100} = 5\frac{1}{3}$ %.

cal viewpoint conclude that very little of our economic growth can be credited to the increase in our capital stock. The same studies indicate that, since capital is only one of several important inputs, a big increase in investment would have a disappointingly small effect on the rate of growth. An increase in the investment-output ratio of three percentage points, as Tobin proposed, would, according to these studies, raise the rate of growth by less than one percent.

Yet without investment, productivity would not grow at all. Clearly we have to renew and reshape old capital if we are to take advantage of the technological advances which account for so much of our growth. Thus investment is needed to modernize the capital stock as well as to maintain or enlarge it. One implication of this new view of investment is that the net rate of return on business investment is substantially higher than had been thought before. Still the major sources of growth seem to lie elsewhere.

Theodore Schultz believes the secret of growth is education. Schultz finds that the capital stock has not been keeping up with output. We seem to need less and less tangible capital. One explanation of this, Schultz acknowledges, is increasing returns to scale: our productivity per man-hour and per unit capital may benefit from the increase in the size of the economy. But the more important explanation, Schultz believes, is that "human capital" has been growing very rapidly—faster than tangible capital and faster even than output—and that this human capital is replacing tangible capital. While tangible capital was about four times larger in 1956 than 1900, the "stock of education"—the value of the resources devoted to the education of the population —rose about eight times in the same period. If we want to grow rapidly in the future, we dare not neglect investment in education.

Schultz goes farther and suggests that there may be "substantial underinvestment" in human beings at the present time. Schultz may very well feel that we have too little of all kinds of capital; however by "underinvestment" he means that we have invested too little in "human capital" *relative* to our enormous investment in tangible capital. He is suggesting that had we invested less in the latter and more in the former, we would have a higher level of productivity.

Gary Becker questions this hypothesis. Presumably most of the benefits of education are reflected in the greater incomes that educated persons in the labor force can earn. But Becker estimates that college students earn a rate of return on their "investment" in a college education of only 9 percent or so (before taxes). Is this better than the rate of return earned by businesses on their tangible capital? Becker estimates that businesses in the early 1950's earned at least 8 percent on their capital (before taxes). And the editor's essay estimates that, when the superior efficiency of modern investments is taken into account, the rate of return on business capital was nearer to 14 percent (at high levels of capacity utilization). So there is still no strong case for the "underinvestment" hypothesis, although the matter is not settled yet.

What advantages has an educated labor force? It is more mobile, faster to learn, more skillful, and better at problem-solving. On the highest plane this problem-solving is called *research*. Presumably research makes a great contribution to technical change. But what kind of research do we need? What is the most efficient allocation of our research personnel? Benton Massell and Richard Nelson look at this question.

They see no need to subsidize or otherwise stimulate industrial research and development. So long as the benefits of industrial research accrue only to the firms that undertake it, we can count on these firms to make correct research decisions.

The core of the policy recommended by Massell and Nelson concerns fundamental or basic research. Here the incentives of private firms are much weaker. Basic research, by its very nature, has a payoff which is difficult to estimate. Characteristically, the benefits of fundamental research, even when successful, are apt to accrue significantly to a large segment of the economy, not simply to the firm undertaking the research. So there is some presumption that private firms, on the whole, neglect basic research from the standpoint of its total social benefits.[5] This justifies government promotion of basic research.

Fritz Machlup ties together some of the ideas of Part Three. Machlup defines certain departments of economic activities. First, there is the *capital goods* department; and second is the

5. These considerations have an implication for Gary Becker's analysis of the value of education. Becker looks at income differentials in assessing

department of *knowledge*—that is, education, basic research, and applied research. Given the level of consumption we want to have, the choice is between "knowledge" and "equipment."

Machlup points out that it is one thing to stress the importance of knowledge in providing the rate of growth we already have. But it is another thing to suggest that technological research should have first claim on additional resources. We do not know yet whether investment in knowledge or investment in equipment has the higher rate of return.

The allocation problem is especially treacherous in the knowledge department. The huge increase in industrial research and development in the past twenty or thirty years, Machlup reasons, has been largely at the cost of basic research and of education. Of course, ultimately we must have basic *and* applied research *and* education; none is much good without the others. But the plight of education today spells a shortage of research manpower tomorrow.

The final contribution, by the President's Council of Economic Advisers, relates these principal instruments of growth to concrete Federal government policies. If we want more of these kinds of investment than it appears private initiative is going to offer, then government must stimulate initiative or make the desired investments.

The tax-credit incentive is a government measure proposed to stimulate private investment. The massive support already given by the Federal government to private research is recalled. And Federal assistance to education is growing in importance. Clearly the area of framing appropriate policy measures to affect growth —and to do so in the least costly, most efficient way—is a critical one in public policy toward growth.

---

the returns from education. The spread between the income of the scientist and manual laborer is just such a differential. But what if the scientist is doing fundamental research? If he is employed by a private firm, that firm is presumably paying him according to his worth to the firm— not to the whole industry or economy which may share the fruits of his research. Becker's method is exactly right only if everyone is paid according to his marginal social productivity.

PART ONE   A New Policy Issue

America Must Grow
WALTER LIPPMANN AND FRANCIS M. BATOR

Walter Lippmann is a political philosopher, economist, and the dean of newspaper columnists. Francis M. Bator is Associate Professor of Economics at the Massachusetts Institute of Technology. This article first appeared in the Saturday Evening Post *at the height of the 1960 Presidential campaign.*

IN RECENT years we have been hearing more and more about the problem of economic growth: that is, whether the American economy, already the biggest and richest in all history, is growing fast enough. What is causing all this talk about economic growth? It is the challenge of the Soviet Union. In the past five years or so we have come gradually to realize that with our growing population we are not producing enough wealth to (1) keep up the race of arms, (2) finance adequately those of our allies and independent neutrals who are very poor and in need of capital to develop their economies, (3) pay for our developing internal needs and (4) enjoy a continually rising standard of private living. Rich as we are, we find that we are not becoming richer fast enough to support successfully all the growing demands that come from these four vital interests.

We have been faced, in truth, with very hard and perhaps even dangerous choices—(1) to let our defenses become vulnerable and insufficient, (2) to let great regions of the world, including Latin America, turn to Moscow for help and for leadership, (3) to stint on schools and hospitals and scientific research and public transportation and on our great cities and on the conservation of our human and natural resources or (4) to levy additional taxes to freeze, and perhaps even to reduce, private consumption in order to free labor and capital for producing missiles and schools.

The pressure of these competing national interests on the Administration and Congress has become very heavy. Increasingly we find ourselves in a jam. We cannot now afford to support adequately all four of our national interests, and yet we cannot hold our place in the world if we skimp on our defense or on foreign aid or on schools or on other essential public needs.

We could, to be sure, pay for them if we were willing to sacrifice a rising standard of living. We could, as in wartime, pay much higher taxes and, to tell the truth, we could still live comparatively well—much better than we lived during World War II and as well as or better than we lived during the Korean War.

But almost nobody wants to do this. Almost nobody wants to reduce, or even to freeze where it is, the American standard of private life. But to go on living better and better, and to wipe out as we go along the large pockets of primitive poverty which still exist, we must either take enormous risks where our vital interests are concerned or we must find a way to speed up our economic growth.

The talk about economic growth is being heard among us because those dangerous choices have been put to us.

THE SOVIET CHALLENGE

We may take September 23, 1949, as the date on which the challenge of the Soviet Union to our primacy as a world power became visible. That was the date when President Truman announced that the Soviet Union had achieved a nuclear explosion. Our monopoly of nuclear weapons had been broken.

The explosion of 1949 announced two interrelated developments which have loomed bigger and bigger through the 'Fifties and now constitute the core of the challenge which confronts us. The explosion of 1949 served notice upon us that in a few years the Soviet Union could become a military power at least our equal and perhaps, if we relaxed, our superior. The explosion put us on notice, too, that the prevailing picture of the Soviet economy as primitive and grossly inefficient was false. It indicated that, just as our nuclear monopoly was broken, so might in the course of time be our pre-eminency in economic power.

If the nuclear explosion of 1949 was the warning that our primacy among the great powers was going to be challenged, the sputnik of 1957 was the alarm bell which should have aroused all Americans out of their habitual sense of security. It did arouse some Americans. It is no accident that the celebrated report on economic growth, which was financed by the Rockefeller Brothers Fund, is called *The Challenge to America* and was published a year or so after sputnik. It is not surprising that the report is dominated by the Soviet military challenge—by the fact that the Soviets appeared to be well on their way to acquiring enough nuclear weapons and missiles seriously to threaten our dangerously vulnerable retaliatory forces.

The Rockefeller report by no means deals only with the military aspects of the challenge. But its central recommendations are strongly colored by the size of the military problem, for armaments are much the biggest burden which the taxpayer has to carry. Spending for national security takes more than half the Federal budget and, more significantly, accounts for something like 85 per cent of total Federal purchases of goods and services—that is, of Federal spending which makes a claim on scarce goods and labor and other services.

If it were not for this military expenditure, the other interests that we have to support would prove to be no problem at all. We could reduce taxes and yet spend the money required for schools, public health and the other civil needs of our people, without stinting private consumption and without incurring the danger of inflation. Even then, we would have to make sure that total demand—private plus public spending—grew fast enough to provide jobs for our ever-growing labor force. But the problem of getting more and more output would not be so urgent. It is because of the size of the military burden that we are compelled to think so hard about the problem of economic growth.

At the Twenty-first Communist Party Congress in 1959, Mr. Khrushchev declared that "the Soviet Union intends to outstrip the United States economically."

The military challenge of the Soviet Union is supported by an industrial economy which is growing rapidly in productive capacity and in its ability to perform sophisticated technological operations—such as, for example, shooting a satellite around the moon.

In our government the responsibility for keeping track of the Soviet economy lies in the Central Intelligence Agency. On the basis of this agency's studies, the director, Mr. Allen W. Dulles, has testified that the total output of the Soviet economy is likely to continue to grow at a rate of about 6 per cent over the next decade, a rate more than twice the recent American rate. And Soviet industrial production, which is so important for military power, is likely to grow even faster. By holding down the private standard of life, the Soviet Government has at least matched us in the amount of resources devoted to military power, to pure and applied science and to the training of engineers and technicians of all kinds.

MEETING THE CHALLENGE

This places us under a very severe competitive challenge. How are we to meet it? We can do so, it would appear, in one of two ways. We can arrest the rise in our private and our public standard of living. Or we must produce more wealth by raising the rate of growth of our economy.

The economists tell us that if, instead of the recent 2.5 per cent, we can maintain an average rate of growth for the next ten years of about 4 per cent, or a little better, we shall be able to support our vital interests and still maintain a rising standard of private life. If we do not succeed in doing this, then we shall have to choose between failure to meet the Soviet challenge—which is unthinkable and would be intolerable—or we shall have to accept a much bleaker, a much less open and hopeful way of life in America. . . .

The things we must do in order to meet the Soviet challenge have already been described, though not in detail. We must have a military establishment which can secure the balance of power. We must play a leading part in helping the rise of the under-developed nations. We must meet the needs of our growing population for schools, hospitals and other essential public facilities.

And we must, if possible, do all these things while maintaining a rising standard of private consumption. We must try to maintain that rising standard both for the comfort and welfare of our own people, and also as a demonstration to the world of the quality and vitality of our social order.

Let us be clear about it. We have the labor, the capital and the know-how to do all that is demanded of us. If we fail, it will be for lack of brains and of determination. For that which is required is nothing revolutionary or unprecedented. It is to raise the average rate of our economic growth from less than 3 per cent, as it has been since the end of the Korean War, to an average of 4 per cent or a little better. If we succeed in doing that, we shall have the means to do what we have to do.

To reach such an average, the rate of growth would have to be more than 4 per cent in very good years to make up for the losses in the slumps. But no one is suggesting that we try to adhere to a rigid, fixed target year by year.

Would a 4 per cent average during the next decade be adequate? It is a much higher rate than the 2.5 per cent we have achieved since the end of the Korean War. But it is less than the 5 per cent which the 1960 Democratic Party platform calls for. It is less, also, than the 5 to 6 per cent which Governor Rockefeller has been advocating. It is substantially less than the growth rate of the Russian economy and it is less also than the recent growth rate of such capitalist nations as West Germany (8 per cent) and France, Italy, Holland, Canada and Mexico— all of which have grown at rates ranging from 4.5 to 5.5 per cent.

Nonetheless, while it would be agreeable to exceed 4 per cent, if one looks at the figures—at the size of the problem—it would appear that 4 per cent will do. With 4 per cent we can meet our needs for defense and for civilian public services as estimated, for instance, by the Rockefeller Brothers Fund Report and still count on an appreciable improvement in the standard of private life.

Let us look only at the totals. As noted previously, if you exclude the transfer payments and include defense, public purchases of goods and services in 1959 came to about $98,000,000,-000. Now consider the Rockefeller Report's two estimates of the public purchase which is required if we are to meet the Soviet challenge and the demands of our vital civilian interests.[1] Minus transfer payments, the low estimate calls for an increase in the total to $134,000,000,000 in 1967, in terms of 1959 prices. The high estimate calls for $161,000,000,000.

These figures show why so many who study the problem are so concerned, indeed excited, about the rate of growth. For suppose we continue to grow at our present slow rate of 2.5 per cent in gross national product per year. Then even the *low* Rockefeller estimate of spending for essential public needs will squeeze our standard of living. We are used to an average increase in private consumption per head of about 1.5 per cent to 2 per cent a year. But if we continue to grow at our present rate and if we are to reach the minimum target set in the Rockefeller report by 1967, then our consumption per head—our private standard of living—would barely grow at all.

Now consider the contrast. Suppose our gross national product grows at a rate of 4 per cent a year. Then we can reach the low Rockefeller target while at the same time our private consumption per person would increase by better than 2 per cent a year —a rate substantially faster than during the recent past. By 1967 real consumption per household could rise from its 1959 level of $6100 to about $7200.

With 4 per cent and the low target, we would have a rich private society. But we might be taking risks with defense, education and our cities. Could we manage the Rockefeller high target for government? With gross national product growing at 4 per cent we could certainly do so—and without much strain. Personal consumption per person would grow at 1.25 per cent a year—not so fast as during the first postwar decade, but only a little more slowly. Personal consumption per household could increase from $6100 to better than $6600.

Is there reason to think that a target rate of 4 per cent is dangerously high? We think it fair to say that the most serious professional students of the matter agree that it is not. True, it is a faster rate than our long-term average of 3.5 per cent. But the period since 1839—from which year the 3.5 per cent is measured —has included a number of deep and prolonged depressions.

1. [See the table of Rockefeller Report projections of public expenditures in 1967 on p. 14. *Editor*]

Also, during most of this period, large-scale research to speed technological advance played a much smaller role than it does today. Moreover, we have in fact enjoyed periods of nearly 4 per cent growth. Between 1889 and 1929 the real gross national product grew at an average rate of 3.7 per cent; and between 1947 and 1956 at 4 per cent.

Nor is there reason to think that 4 per cent growth is very difficult for a capitalistic economy. As we have seen, a number of the capitalist nations of Western Europe have done a great deal better than 4 per cent during the past decade.

GROWTH AS A GOVERNMENTAL GOAL

There are some among us, of course, who think that while 4 per cent is not impossible, it is none of the government's business. Specifically, there are those who believe that the government cannot have a policy to promote growth. And there are those who believe that any policy to stimulate growth will undermine our system of private enterprise.

To those who say that the government cannot affect growth, the answer is that it can and that it does. Thus it can promote growth by varying taxes, the tightness of money and its spending so as to keep total private, plus public, spending in balance with capacity.

It can promote growth by altering taxes to bear more on consumption and less on saving, by permitting rapid amortization and by making money cheaper, so as to shift the composition of spending in favor of private investment and against private consumption.

It can promote growth by using taxes to release resources for public investment. Spending on roads and laboratories, on airports and on urban transport all add to the productive capacity of the economy.

It can promote growth, at least in the longer run, by supporting research, improving the quality of education and promoting public health.

It can promote growth by a number of indirect measures. It can make it easier for people to change jobs and move from areas of labor surplus. It can disseminate information about high-productivity techniques. It can campaign against the more serious rigidities in big business and big labor. It can rationalize its own agricultural program. It can reduce tariffs and allow foreign competition to encourage greater efficiency.

The capacity of the government to promote growth cannot be disputed. The truth is that government cannot be neutral even if it wants to be. By the way it makes use of its traditional instruments of policy, it will inevitably affect growth. Those of us who believe that we must speed up growth are proposing that in making its decisions about taxes and spending, tariffs and interest rates, the government should take into account their effect on growth and exploit its own power for stimulating growth.

What, then, about those who charge that measures to promote growth are alien to the principles of a free economy—that such measures would require a dangerous degree of socialistic interference? Anyone who thinks about this in concrete terms, rather than in the abstract, is bound, we think, to conclude that these fears are unfounded and that there is nothing proposed by Governor Rockefeller and others who are concerned with growth which is not based on orthodox and indeed conservative practices.

The use of taxation to give an incentive to saving and to investment through, for example, liberal amortization allowances, is certainly an old story. The use of private money for public investment to add to our public capital has not been radical since the government used tax money to promote public schools and post offices, roads, harbors and giant dams. The management of taxes and of credit to deflate booms and to reflate slumps has been required by the law of the land for many years. There is nothing about any of this which involves regimentation.

Nor is there any basis to the charge that a policy of deliberate growth is socialism. Socialism involves the public ownership and operation of the means of production, of the mines, the factories and of all public utilities. What we are talking about is the rate of growth of private production in order to support a steady rise in personal consumption and an unavoidable and desirable increase in the amount of goods purchased from private industry by all levels of government.

We are talking about how to pay private contractors to build missiles and aircraft carriers, schools, hospitals and parks—not about how the government can build them. The program we have in mind calls for government purchases from private firms and the hiring of civil servants in a free labor market. Only by an unscrupulous use of language can this be called socialism.

RISING GOVERNMENT SPENDING

What about the concern of many people that the increase in government spending which lies ahead of us will make the government too big a customer in the market place?

Here again we have to look at some figures. In 1959 the share of our gross national product taken by all levels of government was 20.3 per cent. If between now and 1967 the economy grows at an average annual rate of 4 per cent and if government purchases increase to reach the low Rockefeller estimates by 1967, the government share in total output will remain at 20.3 per cent. There would be no change.

On the other hand, if we try for the Rockefeller high estimates, the public share in total output would rise to 24.6 per cent by 1967. Thus, if we decide on the high target, it is true that government purchases which now absorb about one fifth of total output would rise to a little less than one quarter.

A rise from 20.3 per cent to 24.6 per cent is considerable and would have to be watched. But if anyone thinks that this would involve us in a really serious effort, he would do well to look at the World War II figures. In 1943 government purchases absorbed a full 46 per cent of the gross national product.

What is important to remember is that even if we try for the Rockefeller high target, as the authors think we should, and even if we fail to accelerate growth beyond 4 per cent, more than three quarters of all final purchases will still be made by private individuals and private businesses. An economy which is more than 90 per cent in private hands for production and which is more than 75 per cent in private hands for consumption, is overwhelmingly a private economy.

This is all well and good, some will say, but what about spending by the Federal Government and the increasing encroachment by Washington on state and local functions?

Once again it is a good idea to look at the figures. In 1959 total Federal spending came to over $91,000,000,000, of which about $6,000,000,000 went to finance state-local spending; the state-local total was over $47,000,000,000. However, well over half of the Federal total went for national security, which is obviously the Federal Government's business. Federal civilian spending amounted to less than the state-local total. Moreover, most of the money did not divert goods and services from state or local or private use. It consisted instead of grants-in-aid or interest on the debt or social security and veterans' cash benefits. Federal civilian purchases of goods and services, in fact, amounted to only $7,200,000,000, less than 15 per cent of all public nondefense purchases. This is a much smaller share than in 1939–40 (32 per cent) or in 1949 (28 per cent) or even in 1954 (23 per cent). The fact is that in 1959 the Federal Government absorbed less than 1.5 per cent of the total nondefense output of the economy, in contrast to about 4 per cent in 1939 and 2.5 per cent in 1954.

Nor is there cause for alarm as regards the future. While the Rockefeller estimates are not broken down as between Federal and state-local spending, from other comparable estimates it is clear that even if we meet the Rockefeller high targets, no more than the current 15 per cent of public civilian purchases would be Federal. We can meet our public needs without the state and local governments surrendering to Washington.

DEALING WITH INFLATION

We come now to inflation and we may say that if it were not for the fear of inflation, there would be almost no controversy about economic growth. Everybody is in favor of growth. But it is demonstrably harder to hold down inflation in a booming economy than in a sluggish one. With full employment, with demand pressing against capacity, there is always a danger of sellers' markets and of rising wages and prices.

On the other hand, if demand is throttled down to avoid the risk of inflation, it is all too easy to bring about a recession and to halt growth. This poses a perpetual choice for governments and central banks: How to have enough demand to stimulate growth without inflation, and how to stop inflation without bringing on a slump.

There are in theory measures which could contain inflation, to break up the big business monopolies which set prices, to break up the big labor monopolies which force wages higher than the increase in productivity warrants, and to bring about a drastic reduction of the tariff. But we do not expect to see either party take such measures; and we assume, therefore, that we must face the problem of agreements made by big business and by big labor, which raise wages and prices and produce what economists call a cost-push inflation.

The nation will have to work out a policy for dealing with inflationary wage bargains. We ourselves think it unnecessary and, except in wartime, we think it highly undesirable to combat such bargains by fixing wages and prices. But we see no reason why, when big business and big labor are bargaining, the public through the government should not be represented in the negotiations. The government should certainly insist on a judicial finding on the facts in the dispute, it should insist on making public the results of the fact finding and it should generate public opposition against any increase greater than the average rise in labor productivity in the economy as a whole.

No one need pretend that these things are easy to do or that any of us have a simple cure to solve our problems. A higher rate of growth will, it is obvious, not solve all our problems. But the paramount fact is that a great many of our greatest problems cannot be solved without a higher rate of growth.

In truth, this is the central and happy fact of our situation, one which calls for emphasis after these years of defeatist anxiety: We can meet the Soviet challenge, hold our place in the world and take care of our civilian public needs without having to change the fundamental structure of our economy.

Rockefeller Report Projections of Federal, State and Local Government Expenditures in 1967

| | Billions of 1957 Dollars | | |
	1957 Actual	The Range of Estimates for 1967 Low	High
National Security	$ 46.0	$ 60.0	$ 70.0
Defense Department	39.0	49.8	55.9
Military Aid	2.3	3.0	4.5
Economic Aid	1.7	2.7	3.7
Atomic Energy *	2.1	3.0	3.9
Other	.9	1.5	2.0
Education (Including School Construction)	13.0	24.0	30.0
Welfare	20.0	38.5	45.0
Social Insurance and Public Assistance	15.5	31.0	36.0
Health (Including Hospital Construction)	4.5	7.5	9.0
Public Works (Except Schools and Hospitals)	9.5	20.5	27.0
Roads **	4.8	10.5	12.0
Water Supply and Disposal	1.3	2.7	3.5
Urban Renewal	0.7	4.0	7.0
Other	2.7	3.3	4.5
Other	25.5	27.9	31.0
Agriculture	4.7	2.0	2.0
Veterans	4.9	4.9	4.9
Administration ond Operation	15.9	21.0	24.1
Total Government Cash Expenditures	**$114.0**	**$170.9**	**$203.0**

* Includes expenditures by the Atomic Energy Commission on civilian projects.
** $10.5 billion estimate for 1967 is based on current legislation.

[SOURCE: Rockefeller Brothers Fund, *The Challenge to America: Its Economic and Social Aspects*, p. 68].

Economic Growth as a National Goal

HERBERT STEIN AND EDWARD F. DENISON

Herbert Stein is Director of the research staff of the Committee for Economic Development. Edward F. Denison is an economist at the Brookings Institution. Both organizations sponsor research on current economic problems. This essay was part of a longer contribution to the American Assembly symposium on American goals in the 1960's.

THE AMERICAN ECONOMY works well. It produces the highest income per capita ever known, and a rate of growth that raises real income per capita by half from one generation to the next. This income, and its increase, are widely distributed. Economic advance has produced a revolutionary reduction in the hours and burdens of work. Americans have great freedom to use their resources and incomes as they choose. The system is highly responsive to the demands of the people, producing with exceptional efficiency, inventiveness and adaptability the particular goods and services for which a private or public demand is expressed. Unemployment remains a problem, but one so reduced in magnitude since the 1930's as to be qualitatively different.

America and the civilization to which it belongs stand at an historic turning point. They confront a critical danger and inspiring opportunities. The danger is indicated by the phrase "cold war." Among the opportunities are to help the billion people of the under-developed world realize their aspirations, to reduce nationalist and racialist limitations upon man's freedom and horizons, and to push back the frontiers of human knowledge in many directions. Neither avoidance of the danger nor realization of the opportunities *requires* that the American economy work better, although better economic performance would make both objectives easier to attain. Insofar as movement toward these more important goals depends upon the availability of economic resources, the American economy as it is and is likely to be can provide them. It would be tragic if the United States should fall prey to the danger or fail to grasp the opportunities because of preoccupation with the idea that it is not rich enough and needs to become richer faster.

NATIONAL PRODUCTION AND NATIONAL NEEDS

From 1929 to 1957 the total production of goods and services in the United States increased at an average rate of 2.93 per cent per annum. We estimate that if unemployment is kept to about 4 per cent of the labor force, the annual rate of growth from 1957 to 1970 would be 3.27 per cent, and from 1957 to 1980 would be 3.24 per cent. At the estimated rate of growth GNP would be about $709 billion in 1970 and $972 billion in 1980 [at 1957 prices].

This estimate of future growth assumes that no special measures are taken to accelerate growth other than the reduction of unemployment. It is based on an analysis of the probable contribution to growth that will be made by several factors—the number, hours of work, educational attainment and age-sex composition of the labor force, the stock of capital, the increase of knowledge, and others. It assumes, among other things, that the 1970 labor force will be about 19 per cent larger and average annual full-time working hours about 5 per cent shorter than in 1960; that the educational attainment of the labor force will increase sharply; that the capital stock will grow at about the rate indicated by past ratios of saving to national product under prosperous conditions.

Estimates of future growth under conditions of high employment have been made by other students. Some project growth rates similar to ours, others project higher rates. The difference generally lies in the weight given to the relations observed in the long period 1929–57 as compared with a shorter more recent period, especially 1947–1950 or the postwar period inclusive of those dates. This shorter period may be interpreted as evidence that a "New Era" began after the war, in which various factors, notably the advance of technology, will hereafter generate a more rapid rate of growth than previously experienced. Alternatively, since this short period was one of quite low unemployment, it may be interpreted as evidence that high employment by itself makes a very large contribution to the growth rate.

In the space available here we cannot discuss and defend the points of difference between our estimates and others. We would only say that we believe the longer period to be more reliable than a selected shorter period, in the absence of clearer evidence than now exists of a persistent change in some relationship.

The most obvious question to ask about the projected rate of growth is: Will it be enough? In one sense of course the answer is No. The growth of production is the source from which desires for goods and services are satisfied. These desires appear limitless. However fast production may grow, some desires will be left unsatisfied, and many will wish that growth were faster.

However, the rate of growth will not be increased by wishing. Steps will have to be taken to increase it. By and large these steps will involve some cost to someone—otherwise we could assume that they would already have been taken. (Remember that we are discussing the problem of raising the rate of growth above that which would otherwise result at high employment—whatever that rate may be.) The question then is not whether faster growth is desirable but whether it is sufficiently desirable to justify any particular step that might be taken to achieve it.

This question may be concretely illustrated as follows. We estimate that if annual hours of work were to remain at their 1957 level, rather than to decline at the rate we project, our annual rate of growth from 1957 to 1970 would be 3.6 per cent instead of 3.3 per cent. Faster growth is a good thing and reduction of hours of work is a good thing. The question is whether increasing the rate of growth is more important than reducing hours of work. Similar questions can be asked about increasing immigration, or employment of women, or expenditures for education, or taxes for public investment, or tax changes to promote private investment, or expenditures for research.

When the question is put in this way it becomes obvious that the authors of this paper cannot responsibly pretend to answer it. We can try to illuminate the benefits of more rapid growth and indicate the costs of achieving it. But whether the benefits are worth the costs can be answered only by those affected or by those making the decisions. The costs and benefits are not reducible to any common terms that permit their objective measurement and comparison. In the end the decision will have to reflect subjective judgments, and insofar as they are collective decisions they will have to reflect some concensus of subjective judgments.

Whether a collective decision about the rate of growth should be made, through government, is in our opinion a real and serious question. The alternative view is that the desirable rate of growth and the correct means to achieve it are those that would emerge from private decisions. These would inevitably be affected by the action of government in discharging its important functions. But these functions do not include the explicit determination of the rate of growth. We believe that there is much to be said for this position, and we trust that it will receive due weight in public discussion of growth. We do not examine this position here only because it seems more fruitful to use our limited space to indicate what choices are available in the economic system if collective choices are to be made.

How much is growth worth? · If our economy grows at the rate we project, 3.3 per cent per annum, total output (Gross National Product) will be about $710 billion in 1970. If it grows at 4 per cent per annum, GNP in 1970 will be about $780 billion. The value of the higher rate of growth is $70 billion of output in 1970 and corresponding amounts in other years.

How much is this $70 billion worth? Obviously, the answer will depend upon what the $70 billion consists of and what wants it satisfies. If it includes critical defense expenditures, the caloric intake necessary for sustaining the population, the capital assistance that would set the underdeveloped world on the road to growth, then the $70 billion will be of the utmost importance. But anyone can think of possible uses of $70 billion that would be of little importance.

One can conceive of all possible uses of output being ranked in an endless descending series from the most important to the less important, to those of no importance at all, to those of negative value. Ideally, with $710 billion of GNP we would go down from the top of this list through the $710 billion most important uses. If we had another $70 billion of GNP we would take the next most important $70 billion of uses, all of which would be less valuable than any of the first $710 billion. The value of the additional $70 billion would be much less than 10 per cent of the value of the first $710 billion.

It may be that the actual American selection of uses of output does not conform to this pattern. Possibly we select more or less at random from the most important, less important, and unimportant uses. In this case the additional $70 billion of output might be as valuable, dollar for dollar, as the first $710 billion.

There might even be a systematic bias in the process, which causes the less important needs to be satisfied before the more important. If so, the needs satisfied by the additional $70 billion of output would be much more important, on the average, than those satisfied by the first $710 billion.

The importance of more rapid growth depends critically upon how well we allocate our output among our needs. This simply means that if we can count on devoting our expected output to satisfying our most urgent needs, additional output will be only as valuable as the satisfaction of our less urgent needs.

As the authors see it, the key current question about the allocation of output relates to the division between private and public uses. There may be limits upon the amount of public expenditure that keep critical public needs from being met, even though much less important private needs are met. Suppose, for example, that we cannot or will not spend more than 20 per cent of the gross national product for public purposes. If the gross national product in 1970 is $710 billion we can have only $142 billion of public expenditures, even though this may leave unmet many public needs more important than the needs satisfied by some of the $568 billion of private expenditures. The value of raising the GNP would then lie in the additional public expenditures it would permit.

It should be understood that in this paper we have made no evaluation of the need for additional public expenditure. Here we are concerned only to explore the implications for economic growth on the hypothesis that a very large increase of public expenditure is necessary.

There are two main possibilities to be considered. One is that we cannot raise tax rates above their present levels, at least without serious effects upon economic growth. The other is that we *will* not raise tax rates. In either case the yield of the existing tax rates sets a limit to public expenditure, and the only way to raise that expenditure would be to increase the yield of the existing tax rates by increasing the rate of economic growth.

Granted a willingness to raise tax rates, it must be recognized that certain patterns of tax increase might tend to retard the rate of growth. But substantial additions to revenue can be obtained without such an effect. This might involve some combination of (a) increases in the beginning rate of individual income tax (now 20 per cent), (b) a broadening of the income tax base by reduction of exemptions and exclusions and (c) increased taxation of consumption. Such taxation would be burdensome, but this burden is simply that which is implicit in any decision to sacrifice private consumption for public expenditures.

Whether higher public expenditures financed by higher taxes will retard the rate of economic growth depends not only on the character of the taxes but also on the character of the expenditures. If the expenditure increase is heavily weighted with public investment, research, education, and defense programs with a large research content, and if the taxation impinges almost entirely on private consumption, the net effect may be a higher rate of growth.

Even if taxes can be increased without adverse effects upon growth the public and its government representatives may be unwilling to impose the additional taxes. In this case a higher rate of growth would be needed to permit more public expenditures by increasing the yield of the existing tax system.

The authors believe that there are unnecessary obstacles to an increase or decrease of federal taxes. Sharp disagreement over the proper distribution of tax burdens, exaggerated impressions of the consequences of the level and structure of taxes, the complexity of the tax system—all these make a tax increase or decrease excessively difficult. As a result, government expenditures tend to be adjusted to the yield of the existing tax system, even though the best level of expenditure might be higher or lower.

Too much should not be made of this point. At least in this century, no President has been unable to get an increase of taxes when he asked for it to finance expenditures that he described as essential to a vital national interest. Nevertheless, the tendency to regard the yield of the existing tax system as a limit to public expenditures is, we believe, a potentially dangerous obstacle to sound public policy. No law of history assures us that we can get safely through the twentieth century with the yield of the tax system we inherited from the Revenue Acts of 1950 and 1954. The American people should recognize this.

A more rapid rate of economic growth would reduce the importance of this obstacle. But we are doubtful of the possibility of circumventing this obstacle by raising the rate of growth. Many of the steps that might be taken to increase the rate of growth would themselves require higher taxes. Is it likely that, being unable to raise taxes to pay for important public expenditures, we would be able to raise taxes to stimulate growth so that we could pay for these same expenditures? We think not, but we are not experts on what the American people can be persuaded to do. In any case we believe it would be a serious mistake to leave the American people with the impression that the rate of economic growth can be raised to whatever figure is necessary to make the yield of the existing tax system cover all desired public expenditures.

The argument to this point may be summarized as follows: If the national product is wisely used, the contribution of a higher rate of economic growth would be the satisfaction of less critical needs, not of the most critical needs. But the less critical needs are still worth satisfying, and should not be disregarded. They motivate a large part of the work done in this country.

If this country does not allocate its output to the most important uses, it cannot be sure that any specified rate of growth or level of output will satisfy its critical needs. In this case there are two possibilities. One is to increase the rate of growth, which would probably increase the likelihood that important needs would be met. The other is to become more intelligent in recognizing and responding to vital needs. The latter is essential whatever is done about the former. If we are not wise in the use of our resources, we cannot expect the abundance of our resources always to compensate.

The Competition of Soviet Growth · Up to this point we have been discussing the value of more rapid growth as a means of satisfying private or public needs for goods and services. In the present state of the world, rapid growth of the American economy may have an additional value.

Let us postulate this situation. The Soviet economy is now growing at a percentage rate higher than ours. If this should continue, the absolute annual growth of the Soviet economy will overtake our growth (it may already have done so). Although there are strong reasons to believe that the Soviet Union will be unable to maintain a growth rate faster than ours once it has achieved a comparable level of technical efficiency, let us nonetheless assume that it will do so. Suppose further that, despite this, the United States is able to maintain an adequate military establishment, provide for necessary public services and sustain a rate of growth of private income that is satisfactory to the American people individually. Would we then regard our rate of growth as adequate?

This is an extremely difficult question to answer. It requires us to project our imaginations into a totally new economic, political and psychological situation. We, our allies, neutral nations, and the Soviet bloc are all deeply affected by the vision of the United States as by far the world's richest and economically strongest country. It is hard to conceive a world in which this would not be true.

But it seems possible that a change to a situation in which the Soviet economy is generally recognized to be growing faster than ours, not only in percentages but also absolutely, not in spurts but steadily, and is approaching ours in total size, could have profound consequences. It could greatly strengthen the confidence of the Russians in their own system, increase the attraction of the Communist system for the independent, underdeveloped countries, worry our allies about their reliance upon us, and weaken our own morale.

These consequences might not follow. Certainly they are paradoxical on their face. They imply that in order to increase the attraction of our system to populations with average per capita incomes of $100 we, with per capita incomes of $2,000, must become still richer faster. They imply that even though we fully discharge our real obligations to our allies, they will lose confidence in us because we do not choose to raise our personal consumption more rapidly. They imply that the rest of the world will not evaluate us by the standards we choose for ourselves but will compel us to be measured by standards made in Moscow.

Moreover no one really knows what the standards are in the production race upon which world opinion is said to hinge. We do not know whether the Soviet GNP is now one-third of ours or two-thirds of ours, because the composition of their GNP is so different from ours. And it is not clear whether the race is in GNP at all, or in steel production, or in butter consumption per capita. Each side presumably wants to race on its own track and to persuade the world that it is the right track. The outcome may depend as much on the persuasion as on the running.

Nevertheless the possibility described cannot be ignored. Accelerating our pace in the production race is probably a positive factor for our national security. How important a factor it is, the authors cannot pretend to say. This is a question the American people will have to decide on the advice of people more expert than we in the politics and psychology of the cold war. If they should decide that it is important, this would, in our opinion, be the strongest reason for a collective decision to increase the rate of growth.

The costs of accelerating growth must also be considered. We do not do *everything* that might promote our national security. Especially, we want to promote our national security in the most efficient way. Somehow we must judge whether a cost of x spent in accelerating growth will yield more in national security than the same cost spent for weapons, or for foreign aid, or for space exploration, or for many other things that affect our military, political and psychological position in the cold war. Again this is a question that the authors cannot answer. . . .

CHOOSING AMONG GOALS

Economic growth is a good thing, and it is tempting to elevate any good thing to the state of a goal of national policy. The main point of our paper is that the establishment of such a goal is wise only if the benefits of the "good thing" are worth its costs. We have neither invented nor discovered the costs. In fact, we suppose that consciousness of these costs has weighed in the decisions not to undertake the measures that might have given us more rapid growth in the past.

We should refer here to one kind of benefit and one kind of cost that we have not mentioned but that may be very important. There may be value in having a "national goal" aside from the benefits of achieving any particular goal and almost without regard to what the goal is. The goal may be inspiring, give "point" to life, and serve as a common bond holding the society together. This may be a benefit even though at the present stage of history our psychological need would be better served by a goal less materialistic and less parochial than the growth of the American economy.

There is a limit to the number of goals that the American people or any people can pursue, the number of crusades they can engage in. There is a limit to our supply of leadership for "pointing the way" and to the supply of attention and followership. In this sense, any goal is proposed at the expense of others that are or might have been advanced, and the cost of elevating accelerated economic growth to the front rank of goals is that something else is deprived of that position. The number of goals calling for our attention is large—to help set the under-developed world on the path of economic progress, to reduce the barriers of nationalism and racialism, to strengthen our national security, to improve the lives we lead with our immense flow of goods and services, to set a floor of economic security and welfare for all. We need not feel guilty of negativism or passivity if we decide that accelerating growth is not one of our most critical needs.

In closing, the authors repeat what was said at the outset. We do not, in this paper, attempt to decide what the public attitude toward the rate of growth should be. This is a question that the people must decide, referring to the kinds of considerations discussed here but also in the end expressing their own values, their own views of what is worth what.

United States Growth: What, Why, How

W. ALLEN WALLIS

W. Allen Wallis, formerly Professor of Economics and Statistics at the University of Chicago, is now President of the University of Rochester. He presented this statement at the Third Annual Loeb Dinner for Economic and Business Journalists in June, 1960. At that time he was Special Assistant to President Eisenhower.

WHAT IS ECONOMIC GROWTH?

GENERALLY, PEOPLE think of economic growth as an increasing supply of goods and services. This is all right as far as it goes, but it doesn't go very far. As population increases, a larger supply of goods and services is needed to maintain a constant level of output. An economy may get bigger—or "grow" in an absolute sense, perhaps even as a world power—without adding to individual welfare. Obviously, growth must involve rising levels of *per capita* output if it is to mean increased welfare.

But this is not all. Growth in any meaningful sense must mean not just more things, but more things that are useful and that people want. Today we produce such things as automobiles, television sets, and missiles, instead of surreys, stereopticons, and cannon balls. Evolution in the composition of output is as much a part of economic growth as is expansion of the volume of output. Similarly, if growth is to be meaningful the output must be well distributed among all the people.

In our economy, changes in the composition of output reflect the free choices of the people, and the valuation of the output reflects the values placed on goods and services through voluntary purchases and sales. Private output conforms to choices made in the market, and public output to choices made through political processes by freely elected representatives. In a centralized economy, both private and public output reflect the choices and values of the authorities, and the values placed on goods and services also represent authoritarian decisions. There is no valid criterion of the extent to which the nominal "growth" achieved by a centralized economy is meaningful growth in terms of the aspirations and desires of the people. Furthermore, with centralized economic authority the benefits of growth need not be distributed widely. Total and per capita output can rise, while the living levels of the masses are rising little or not at all.

Clearly, true growth must refer to economic welfare. This means we must consider not only goods and services but non-material aspects of growth. As our productive capacities have risen, we have chosen to take part of our growth in the form of leisure and improved working conditions. In fact, an economy could be growing even though output per capita were stable, if at the same time the amount of time and effort needed to produce that output were declining.

If the concept of growth is complex and elusive, as I have been trying to indicate that it is, the problem of measuring growth is fearsome. Not only do we lack adequate data, but the qualitative and non-material aspects of growth are impossible to quantify. A confession of St. Augustine more than 1500 years ago about the concept of time ought to be repeated daily by all who purport to measure economic growth: "For so it is, oh Lord my God, I measure it; but what it is that I measure I do not know."

Six of the most common gauges of economic growth are the percentage rates of increase in

(1) real Gross National Product, that is, GNP adjusted for price changes;
(2) real GNP per capita;
(3) industrial production;
(4) output per man-hour worked;
(5) output per unit of labor and capital combined; and
(6) real disposable personal income per capita.

Before considering what each of these gauges appears to show, let us consider certain major shortcomings that seriously limit what any of them really show. These ubiquitous flaws, which create troubles for anyone trying to compare growth rates between countries or between times for a given country, are:

(1) deficiencies of data,
(2) vagaries of valuation,
(3) aberrations of averages, and
(4) treacheries of timing.

About the deficiencies of data I will say little, except that the basic figures on GNP or industrial production even for this country—and ours are the best in the world—involve liberal use of estimation and guesstimation, of interpolation and extrapolation, of approximation and adjustment. With respect to Russian data, it is hardly better than conjecture at many crucial points.

The valuation problem I have already alluded to. The list of things produced includes such heterogeneous products as apples, nuts, bolts, cloth, appendectomies, tractors, missiles, financial writing, and speeches. To measure the list by a single number it is necessary to put a value on each item. In a market economy, we can value most things by prices people voluntarily pay and accept. Even in our economy, however, a large and increasing share of output is governmental, and can be valued only in terms of things used up. But just using up something by no means guarantees that an equal value is created; sometimes it is more, too often it is less.

U.S.–U.S.S.R. Comparisons · The magnitude of the valuation problem is shown by the comparatively simple problem of comparing Russian GNP with ours. The two lists of products must be valued by the same prices, otherwise the comparison will reflect differences in prices, not just differences in GNP. If Russian prices are applied to their output and to ours, our GNP is nearly four times theirs. If American prices are applied to the outputs of both countries, we are only twice their size. Russian GNP for 1955 is commonly described as 40 per cent of ours. This results from splitting the difference, but the difference that is split is not between two and four, which would give three, but between 27 per cent and 53 per cent, which are the two estimates of Russian GNP as a percentage of ours.

Averages can be tricky, and every one of the growth measures is an average of divergent rates of growth prevailing in different parts of the economy. It is possible, for example, for the overall average to go up even if every separate part is constant or even declining. To see that this is possible, suppose that a country has half its economy in agriculture, and that growth is slower in agriculture than in the other half of the economy (both these things are true of Russia). The average rate of growth for the whole economy will be half-way between the rate for agriculture and the rate for nonagriculture. Now suppose that the economy changes, and the nonagricultural segment is larger than the agricultural. Even if the rate of growth stays the same in both agriculture and nonagriculture, the new average rate of growth for the whole economy will be nearer the nonagricultural than the agricultural rate, and therefore higher than before. This kind of thing is in fact happening in Russia. In the United States, on the other hand, the opposite is happening. Agriculture here has an extraordinarily large rate of growth, so we are able to shift resources into things like services where growth is slower; and this pulls down the figures on our average rate of growth, even though the change is obviously a good thing. It would be possible for our rate of growth to be higher than the Russian rate in every part of the economy, yet for our average rate to be less than theirs.

Another affliction of our measures of growth is the problem of a proper time-span, whatever criterion is used. Like every kind of growth, economic growth proceeds at an uneven pace. Measurements must be made at times far enough apart to average out seasonal, cyclical, and erratic fluctuations. A fictitiously high rate will result if we start at a cyclical trough and end at a peak, or a fictitiously low rate if we go from a peak to a trough. For similar reasons, the periods used for measuring growth must not begin or end at the peak of a war boom or at the trough of a post-war reconversion.

The treacheries of timing are especially hazardous in comparing growth rates of different countries. For the United States, 1948 to 1957 is a valid peak-to-peak period for measuring growth. For some other country, however, it may be a peak-to-trough or a trough-to-peak period. Comparisons covering the same period for two countries may, therefore, be misleading,

THE HISTORICAL RECORD

All these difficulties mean, not that measurements of growth are futile and fruitless, but that to interpret them requires considerable care, skill, judgment, objectivity, and sophistication about both economics and statistics. Let us proceed to survey the principal measures of growth, paying particular attention to the recent record in relation to the long term record.

Real Gross National Product from 1909 to 1957 grew at an annual compound rate of 2.9 per cent per year. The long-run growth trend has been fairly stable in spite of large departures above and below it. Between 1948 and 1957, the annual rate of growh in total real production was 3.8 per cent, somewhat higher than the long-run rate.

Real GNP Per Capita. From 1909 to 1957 the annual rate of increase in real GNP per capita was 1.5 per cent. From 1948 to 1957 the rate was 2.0 per cent per year, again somewhat higher.

Industrial production, as measured by the Federal Reserve Board Index, increased from 1919 (when the index begins) to 1957 at an average annual rate of 3.7 per cent. Between 1948 and 1957 the annual rate of increase was 4.4 per cent, a little higher, but within the range of statistical variation that characterizes this series.

Real private output per man hour worked increased from 1889 to 1957 at an average annual rate of 2.0 per cent. From 1948 to 1957 the rate was 3.1 per cent, or about 50 per cent higher.

Real output per unit of labor and capital combined, useful as a measure of overall efficiency, increased from 1889 to 1957 at an average annual rate of 1.7 per cent. From 1948 to 1957 the annual rate of increase was 2.4 per cent, about 40 per cent higher.

Real disposable personal income per capita measures the income available to individuals, after taxes, to use as they please. The annual rate of increase from 1929 (when the data begin) to 1957 was 1.6 per cent, a rate pulled down by depression and pushed up by war booms. From 1948 to 1957 the average annual rate of increase was 1.9 per cent, despite high taxation and rapid population increase.

There are many other indicators of growth: length of the work week, or levels of education, for example. But the six indices that we have looked at suffice to illustrate the nature of the problems in answering the question: What is Economic Growth?

Even this brief look at the record shows the falsity of careless allegations that our economy is slowing down. The recent record, as best we are able to read it at such close range, is very good when judged by historical standards. Indeed, considering the great changes that have taken place and the major adjustments that the economy has made with flexibility and resiliency during the past fifteen years, the record is one which should renew our faith in the vitality of our system. Perhaps we should, can, and will grow faster and better; but that is the "to be continued" part of our growth story.

WHY GROW?—ECONOMIC GROWTH AS A POLICY GOAL

Economic growth has been an important goal of our national policy since the founding of the Republic. It remains an important goal, in no way diminished by our remarkable progress. Indeed, economic growth has recently become a political rallying cry, accompanied sometimes by demands that the government revert to the mercantilist policies by which economic growth was sought in the 17th and 18th centuries.

The issue of economic growth has entered the arena of contemporary politics through a course which has characterized many issues in the past quarter of a century. That is that after we have gotten over the hill by private endeavors, and are on our way at a brisk pace, urgent demands arise that the government expedite and direct us.

Characteristically, individuals, private institutions, or general social forces break the paths and provide the initial momentum. Once the vision of an important goal gains currency, and once we are on our way toward attaining it, suddenly we become impatient for a magic carpet to put us there instantly. Our impatience is exploited by those promoting various political schemes. Some of these schemes have become as wilted and shabby as the proverbial saloon sandwich, as they are pushed decade after decade as means to reach whatever goals have most recently come over the horizon or are most rapidly being attained through private forces.

Much of the current emphasis on economic growth is of this character. All sorts of plans are put forth under the banner of growth, with little or no analysis of the way they might promote growth—except growth in Federal spending. The same spending plans, on the other hand, are often described as reasons for wanting growth. We could afford the spending, the argument runs, if we only had growth; and the implication is that those who paint these glowing pictures of what growth could do to expand Federal spending somehow have the key to growth.

The fact that too many of the considerations raised in discussions of growth cannot be taken seriously should not blind us to the fact that there are a number of important considerations that merit close examination.

The Soviet Threat is one of these. The Soviet threat is real and has many points of thrust. It would be perilous to underestimate the danger. But how is it related to our own economic growth? Some people fear that the Russians will "catch up" to us someday and so fulfill the Khrushchev boast about burying us. Others fear that rapid Soviet growth will increase Russian military potential so greatly as to jeopardize the free world's defenses. Still others fear possible adverse "demonstration effects" of rapid Soviet development—that underdeveloped and uncommitted nations will turn to communism as a way of achieving national strength, politically and economically. All these fears merit sober consideration—more consideration than can be given to them here.

First, it should be pointed out that we have a commanding lead over Russia in terms of both total and per capita output. Even if Russian growth rates continue higher than ours, the absolute gap between us will continue to *increase* for some time to come.

Second, we don't know how large the gap really is—except that it is large. As was mentioned earlier, international comparisons, even if we had good data, are a difficult and unrewarding business. We don't know whether Russian GNP is one-half of ours or one-quarter of ours.

Third, international comparisons of rates of growth can be even more misleading than comparisons of levels of output. The Russians, starting from a lower economic base and in a period of postwar reconstruction, should be expected to have a fairly high percentage rate of expansion. Moreover, they are able to take over the accumulated technology already developed and exploited elsewhere. Furthermore, they are transferring masses of people out of low productivity employment in agriculture to industry with its more highly valued output per man hour. They still have approximately 50 per cent of their labor force in agriculture; we have only about 8 per cent. Our employment is expanding in services, where improvements in output per man hour are slow and limited. In other words, Russian growth is more rapid because they are still in the area where improvement is easy and the way has been shown, whereas we are more heavily involved in the difficult tasks of expanding productivity in medicine, journalism, education, engineering, and other services.

In short, there is no possibility that the Russian economy will overtake ours, at any time in the visible future—certainly not in this century. We should not begrudge the Russian people whatever rise they may achieve in their material levels of well-being in return for the privation and hardships they have suffered in the name of economic growth.

Even the "demonstration effects" of Russian economic expansion may be vastly overemphasized. While her 6 to 8 per cent annual rate of growth in total production in recent years may seem impressive, other countries not under communist domination have and are doing better. The economic progress of West Germany, Japan, and Mexico, for example, is far more striking. As a matter of fact, Russia itself grew faster under the Czars during the decade before the First World War.

Unmet Social Needs is a slogan we hear these days as a call for accelerated growth. According to this argument, if we grow faster we will be better able to provide a greater variety of public services and to eliminate what we now regard as poverty.

One of the more pretentious versions of the "needs" argument is that we have shameful public squalor in the midst of vulgar private opulence. This argument has a strong authoritarian smell, an odor of desire to enforce the advocates' tastes on others through governmental machinery. The argument about "public squalor" would be laughed out of court if confronted with the facts of the past decade on construction of schools, improvements in teachers' salaries, super-highways built, increases in the support of research, expansion in aid to the needy, diseases conquered, urban redevelopment, hospitals built, or indeed almost anything else. Growth in public services has been enormous in the past decade. The unmet-social-needers resort to pointing out plaintively that we don't yet have everything that they think we should want, and to lamenting that private opulence dulls interest in social revolution.

The public squalor argument is, in fact, simply this decade's battlecry of socialism, which—intellectually bankrupt after more than a century of seeing one after another of its arguments for socializing the *means* of production demolished—now seeks to socialize the *results* of production.

Aiding the Economic Development of Other Nations is another reason often advanced for trying to accelerate our own rate of growth. This is a laudable and continuing goal of public policy. But it does not follow that increasing our own rate of growth and raising our own level of living will have much influence on the rate of economic progress elsewhere.

The problems of world economic development are formidable. The pressure of population on arable land, the extremes of ignorance in many underdeveloped countries, the diversity of languages, cultures, and political institutions—these and many other economic and social factors are far more important than the direct and indirect aid that we can give. This is not to underestimate the significant contribution that our foreign aid, investment, and technology can make to world development. But what we can achieve depends primarily upon how we allocate our resources to various ends, and on the kinds of international and domestic policies we pursue, rather than on variations in our own rate of growth. Our import and export policies, for example, are vastly more important to underdeveloped countries than whether our GNP grows at 2 per cent or 5 per cent per year.

The Real Growth Imperatives arise from the fact that a strong economy is a growing economy. An economy with a high per capita income such as ours generates a large volume of private saving which must flow into capital accumulation if the economy is to sustain itself. In other words, the continued vitality of the system requires growth.

But beyond such technical matters, we desire growth to promote our private ends and national purposes. It is that simple; we want growth because it enlarges the opportunities of our children, because it expands our capacities to pursue goals of our own choosing, because it increases the range of choices open to us, because it is a rewarding outlet for our creative energies and imagination, because achievement invigorates and stimulates. In short, through economic growth we lead richer and fuller lives.

Moreover, we desire growth for the preservation of our way of life. By continued growth we demonstrate to ourselves, and perhaps to the world, that our system of free enterprise and representative government is indeed strong and able to fulfill rising aspirations and to enhance the dignity of free men. We need to grow to demonstrate that our system is not headed for inevitable collapse, but will survive even in a world of oppression and hostility.

HOW TO GROW

For a variety of reasons there is general agreement that economic growth is an important goal of economic policy. But there is disagreement over the relative importance of growth as compared with other goals and even more disagreement over the means by which growth should be pursued.

Growth is only one of several major goals of economic policy. Economic freedom, stability of employment, stability of the general price level, economic efficiency, and economic security all are important. Properly conceived and pursued, economic growth is compatible with all these other goals; but it becomes incompatible when pursued too ardently or by inappropriate means. Policies to promote growth or any other goal must reflect a compromise among competing goals.

Growth entails certain costs, and attempts to achieve greatly accelerated statistical growth rates may be costly in terms of human hardship. New machines may reduce prematurely not only the value of old machines but also the value of human skills acquired through long training and experience. New products may reduce the incomes of those producing old products. New industries in new locations may uproot homes and communities near old industries. Unless the costs of economic growth are equitably distributed, it is only reasonable to expect strong resistance to growth and its accompanying changes.

To get high rates of growth through more rapid capital accumulation means that people must save more, either voluntarily or by compulsion. In the Soviet Union people are forced to sacrifice current consumption and liberty to meet targets of capital formation imposed by the authorities. As much as Americans want economic growth, compulsions and depressed levels of consumption are costs which they would not willingly pay except in dire emergency.

A great variety of recipes for growth are in current vogue. Most of them are hackneyed antiques, spruced up a bit with new phrases and served under new names. In the main, these recipes represent two fundamentally different approaches: mercantilism and economic liberalism.

In many ways the debate about economic growth today is similar to the great debate two centuries ago over how best to promote the wealth of nations. The mercantilist approach of the 17th and 18th centuries was an engineering approach. The government by detailed design and elaborate regulation of economic life attempted to impose a coordinated plan of growth on society. Sumptuary laws to prevent frippery and waste, public monopolies to channel investment wisely, detailed regulation of labor and trade—all these were part of the scheme of things. Mercantilism gave way to economic liberalism—a biological approach to growth with the government cultivating growth, not imposing it.

The great success of the biological approach, especially in Great Britain and the United States, is a matter of historical record. It remains to be seen whether our basically liberal approach will give way to a rising tide of mercantilist reaction.

Today one school of thought, the modern mercantilists, says that the government should create growth by massive increases in the quantity and diversity of government services and activity— in short, that government should force growth on the economy. This approach also involves forcing people to save more either through taxes or through inflation, in order to divert resources into collective use.

The opposite school of thought, the supporters of an open society, holds that the kinds and levels of public services should be determined on the basis of what we really want government to produce, that each governmental activity should be justified either on cost-benefit principles or on sound grounds of social responsibility, and that government can best promote growth by policies which release and give effect to the creative energies of private citizens.

While the factors that determine percentage rates of growth over a span of years are not fully understood, the success of past growth efforts and accumulated economic knowledge do tell us a good deal about the conditions of economic progress and how the government can best cultivate growth.

The underlying forces that promote national economic growth are basically the same as those that account for the economic progress of individuals. An individual's desire for a higher and more secure standard of living for himself and for his family is the basic stimulus. To this end he studies, plans, works, saves, and invests. He searches out new ways of doing things, and develops new techniques and processes. Hence, one of the most effective means of stimulating economic growth—and at the same time one of our fundamental objectives in seeking economic growth—is to provide expanding opportunities for every individual to realize his own potentialities to the utmost and to open wider vistas for his children; to encourage initiative, independence, and integrity; to preserve and enlarge the moral worth of the individual; and to approach more closely to our ideals of personal freedom, justice and fair play, broad and equal opportunity, the rule of law, and mutual respect and charity.

Growth requires a flexible and adaptable economic system with freedom to experiment. New industries must spring up, and others must decline. New methods must be accepted and old ones discarded. Labor and capital must shift easily and cooperatively in response to economic rewards and penalties. The combination of an abundant flow of new ideas, a willingness to take risks, and the speedy adoption of successful new methods is a condition for a high rate of growth.

The translation of new ideas into practical processes is speeded by a high rate of saving, through which new equipment can be financed and put into use. Saving also contributes to growth even where new methods are not involved, since it makes possible a larger stock of plant and equipment, housing, and other physical capital, which add to our potential supply of goods and services. In this way, the prudence and responsible foresight of people in providing for future needs makes an essential contribution to our growth.

All of this requires an economic environment that can be brought about and maintained only by positive and progressive governmental actions. The government has a two-fold function in promoting growth. First, it must provide a legal and institutional climate conducive to private economic progress. Second, the government must provide various public services and facilities which, while valuable to the nation as a whole, do not offer sufficient rewards to induce private producers to provide them for sale, or do not offer sufficient direct benefits to induce private individuals to buy them.

We are in the midst of a great national debate over economic growth. But until we understand what growth is, why it is an important policy goal, and how it can be achieved within a framework of economic and political freedom, the debate will range over many false and confused issues.

True growth in economic welfare involves both material and nonmaterial benefits, widely diffused. True growth must conform to the values and aspirations of a free people. The "right" or optimum rate of growth is that rate which conforms to the voluntary choices of the people, rather than a rate obtained by coercion, compulsion, or excessive social costs. The rate of growth can be increased by improving the efficiency of the economic system and by pursuing wise public policies to create a favorable environment for growth.

The future chapters of our story of economic growth are still to be written. We can be confident that these chapters will be happy ones if we have the wit and wisdom to preserve and strengthen the forces of progress that have produced in America an abundant economy, a great nation, and a free people.

Public Responsibility for Growth and Stability

PAUL A. SAMUELSON

Paul A. Samuelson is Professor of Economics at the Massachusetts Institute of Technology. A widely known theorist, he frequently testifies at Congressional hearings on government economic policy. The present essay, originally entitled "The New Look in Tax and Fiscal Policy," appeared in Federal Tax Policy for Growth and Stability, *a compendium of contributions by panelists before a subcommittee of the Joint Economic Committee in 1956.*

THERE IS much talk about taxes. When I flick on the dial of my radio in the morning, I hear a Congressman quoted on how our high level of taxes is ruining the Nation. Scratch the barber who cuts my hair and you find a philosopher ready to prescribe for the Nation's monetary ills.

This is as it should be. We expect sweeping statements in a democracy. Yet such sweeping statements have almost no validity from a scientific point of view. Campaign oratory aside, the more assuredly a man asserts the direction along which salvation is alone to be found, the more patently he advertises himself as an incompetent or a charlatan.

The plain truth is this, and it is known to anyone who has looked into the matter: The science of economics does not provide simple answers to complex social problems. It does not validate the view of the man who thinks the world is going to hell, nor the view of his fellow idiot that ours is the best of all possible tax systems. Quite the contrary, economists would indeed be useless if any sensible man could quickly infer for himself simple answers to the big policy questions of fiscal policy. No need then to feed economists while they make learned studies of the obvious. It is precisely because public policy in the tax and expenditure area is so complex that we find it absolutely indispensable to invest thousands of man-years of scholarly time in scholarly economic research in these areas.

COMPETING GOALS

Turning now to the goals of any tax system, we can ask: What tax structure will give us the most rapid rate of growth? What tax system will give us the highest current standard of living? What tax structure will make our system most immune to the ups and downs in employment and prices that make American families insecure? What tax structure will realize most closely the community's sense of fairness and equity? What tax structure will maximize the efficiency with which we produce what our citizens most want?

Upon careful thought it will be obvious that there cannot exist a tax system which will simultaneously maximize these five quite different goals of social life.

It is easy to see that high current living standards and rapid growth of our ability to produce are conflicting ends: you have only to look at a collectivized society like the Soviet Union, which decides to sacrifice consumption levels of the current generation in favor of a crash program of industrialization; you have only to reflect that historically in the slums of Manchester working families might have lived longer in the 19th century if England and the other nations had during the industrial revolution slowed down their rates of material progress; you have only to consider the problem of conserving scarce exhaustible natural resources to realize that every society must all the time be giving up higher future resource potentials in favor of keeping current generation consumption, as high as it is.

You can imagine a society that decides to devote its income in excess of the bare physiological existence level 100 per cent to capital formation. You can imagine it—but there never has been such a society. Nor would any of us want to live in such a one. It should be obvious, therefore, that no sane person would ever seek a tax program which literally maximized our rate of economic growth. It is just as obvious that no sane person would want to maximize present living levels if this meant eating up all our capital on a consumption bender that would leave us an impoverished nation.

There is no need to go through all the other pairs of the five listed goals to show their partial incompatibility. If we are willing to frame a tax system that strongly favors thrifty men of wealth, we may thereby be able to add to our rate of current growth; if we encourage a gentle rate of inflation, we may be able to increase the profits in the hands of the quick-reacting businessman, perhaps thereby stepping up our rate of growth. So it goes, and one could easily work through the other permutations and combinations.

But not all of our five goals are necessarily competing. Some when you realize them, help you to realize the others. If we succeed in doing away with the great depressions that have dogged the economic record, we may thereby add to our rate of growth. If we shape a graduated tax system that enables lower income groups to maintain minimum standards of life, we may ease the task of stabilizing business activity. If we replace distorting taxes by less distorting alternatives, the fruits of the resulting more efficient production can add to our current consumption and to our rate of progress in capital formation.

I shall not prolong the discussion of the degree to which the diverse goals of tax policy are competing or complementary. For we can formulate proper policies without having to measure these important, but complicated, relationships.

IMPLEMENTING COMMUNITY PREFERENCES

Upon being told by the economist that it is absurd for Congress to aim at the most rapid rate of growth possible and that it is equally absurd for Congress to aim at the highest possible current level of consumption, the policymaker may be tempted to say: "I understand that. Won't you therefore as an economist advise us as to just what is the best possible compromise between these extremes?"

A good question but, unfortunately, not one that the expert economist can pretend to give a unique answer to. If he is honest, he must reply: "The American people must look into their own hearts and decide on what they consider to be the best compromise rate of growth."

Just because I have advanced degrees in economics and have written numerous esoteric works in the field, I am not thereby empowered to let my personal feelings, as to how much the present generation ought to sacrifice in favor of generations to come, become a prescription for society. It would be as presumptuous for me to offer such specific advice as to let my family's notions about dental care determine how much the typical American family ought to spend on toothpaste. But it is legitimate for me as an economist to say this: *Whatever rate of capital formation the American people want to have, the American system can, by proper choice of fiscal and monetary programs, contrive to do.* This can be shown by an example.

Suppose the vast majority of the American people look into the future or across the Iron Curtain at the rate of progress of others. Suppose they decide that we ought to have a more rapid rate of capital formation and technological development than we have been having recently. Then the economist knows this can be brought into being (a) by means of an expansionary monetary policy that makes investment funds cheaper and easier to get. Admittedly, such an expanded investment program will tend, if it impinges on an employment situation that is already full and on a price level that is already stationary, to create inflationary price pressures and over-full employment—unless something is done about it. What would have to be done about this inflationary pressure? Clearly (b) a tight fiscal policy would be needed to offset the expansionary monetary policy: By raising taxes relative to expenditure, we would reduce the share of consumption out of our full employment income, releasing in this way the real resources needed for investment.

From these remarks it will be clear that economic science is not only neutral as to the question of the desired rate of capital accumulation—it is also neutral as to the ability of the economy to realize any decided-on rate of capital formation.

I repeat: With proper fiscal and monetary policies, our economy can have full employment and whatever rate of capital formation and growth it wants.

I want to cap the daring doctrine that an economy can have the rate of capital formation it wants with a doctrine that may seem even more shocking. Naturally, I cannot here develop all of the underlying reasoning, nor give all the needed qualifications. But I do in advance want to stress the earnestness with which I put it forward, and to underline that it does spring from careful use of the best modern analyses of economics that scholars here and abroad have over the years been able to attain.[1] The doctrine goes as follows:

1. [Samuelson has elsewhere described that analysis as a *neoclassical synthesis* of modern income determination theory and the truths of classical capital theory. *Editor.*]

A community can have full employment, can at the same time have the rate of capital formation it wants, and can accomplish all this compatibly with the degree of income redistribution taxation it ethically desires.

This is not the place to give a detailed proof of the correctness of this general proposition. It will suffice to illustrate it with two extreme examples.

In the first, suppose that we desire a much higher rate of capital formation but stipulate that it is to be achieved by a tax structure that favors low-income families rather than high-income. How can this be accomplished? It requires us to have an active expansionary policy (open-market operations, lowering of reserve requirements, lowered rediscount rates, governmental credit agencies of the FHA and RFC type if desired) which will stimulate investment spending. However, with our taxes bearing relatively lightly on the ready-spending poor, consumption will tend to be high at the same time that investment is high. To obviate the resulting inflationary pressure, an increase in the overall tax take with an overly balanced budget [i.e., budgetary surplus] would be needed.

Alternatively, suppose the community wants a higher level of current consumption and has no wish to make significant redistributions away from the relatively well-to-do and toward the lower income groups. Then a tighter money policy that holds down investment would have to be combined with a fiscal policy of light taxation relative to expenditure. But note that in this case, as in the one just above, any qualitative mix of the tax structure can be offset in its effects by appropriate changes in the overall budget level and in the accompanying monetary policy.

A SOBERING PUBLIC RESPONSIBILITY

Modern societies necessarily are pursuing monetary and fiscal policies. These policies interact with private thrift to shape the pattern of high employment consumption and investment. Hence it is these public policies that determine to an important degree how fast society builds up its capital. This power over the community's rate of capital formation should constitute a sobering responsibility for the voters in any modern democracy.

PART TWO   Outlook for the "Economic Race"

Comparisons of United States and USSR National Output: Some Rules of the Game

ABRAHAM S. BECKER

Abraham Becker is an economist at the RAND Corporation. RAND is a research organization under contract to a number of government agencies which brings together scientists from a variety of disciplines to work on problems related to national security. Becker's article first appeared in World Politics, *October 1960.*

How LARGE is the Soviet gross national product (GNP) relative to our own? A third as large? Half? Two-thirds? Which of the estimates is correct? As the unique solution, none of them, unfortunately. Nor need we search for other numbers: these are probably the best of the lot, and in any case, the reply would be the same. The problem is not one of data, or of definitions, or of estimating methods. Such problems do exist and present difficulties of their own, but the inescapable and immovable barrier to the unique solution in US–USSR national output comparisons is the crucial fact of differences in the structures of the American and Soviet economies. In general, in comparisons of different economies or of the same economy at different times, diverse structures create what the economist calls an "index-number problem." The worst of it is, the "problem" is insoluble.

All of this is old hat to many students of the Soviet economy and to economists generally. Relegated to performing on the back courts before a limited audience in the know, those concerned with international comparisons were used to playing the game according to rules which have it that a single ratio is at best never more than a half-truth and two ratios can be equally true. However, Soviet-American output comparisons have now become a mass spectator sport, played before an American public that shows signs of being disturbed by the course of the "industrial race" proclaimed by Khrushchev and is anxious to get at the "truth." Unfortunately, in the new popular game of US–USSR comparisons, the rules, which are direct corollaries of the index-number problem, are often more honored in the breach than the observance. New to the game, the public is understandably vague about the rules. Many of the participants, on the other hand, are certainly familiar with the rule-book but are reluctant to undertake what they feel will be difficult explanations.

But to leave matters as they stand can only do our side a disservice, for, as this article proposes to show, a prerequisite to public understanding of where we stand in the economic competition with the Soviet Union is observance of a few critical rules in framing comparisons of the United States and Soviet economies. In redefining these few rules, perhaps it will be possible to demonstrate at the same time that the required explanations are considerably less difficult than is commonly feared.

THE INDEX-NUMBER PROBLEM

It may be helpful to begin with a brief restatement of the index-number problem as it concerns us here. In the example below, using arbitrarily chosen numbers, the national product of the USSR and the United States is assumed to be composed of only the output of guns and butter. The prices per unit, quantities, and values produced in each country are shown in Table 1.

TABLE 1

	USSR			UNITED STATES		
	Price per unit, rubles	Quantity, units	Value of output, rubles	Price per unit, dollars	Quantity, units	Value of output, dollars
Guns	50	100	5,000	10	200	2,000
Butter	100	10	1,000	2	1,500	3,000
National product			R6,000			$5,000

The national product of the USSR is composed of 5,000 rubles of guns and 1,000 rubles of butter, while the United States produces $3,000 of butter and $2,000 of guns. How large is the Soviet national product relative to that of the United States? We cannot compare rubles and dollars directly but must attempt to translate one of the monetary units into the other: we must convert rubles to dollars and then compare two dollar magnitudes, or convert dollars to rubles and compare two ruble magnitudes.

We may affect the conversion by asking, in turn: (a) What is the value of the quantities produced in the USSR *at US prices*, and how does this dollar sum compare with the dollar value of US national product? (b) What is the value of the quantities produced in the United States *at USSR prices*, and how does this ruble sum compare with the ruble value of USSR national product?

The results of these two computations are given in Table 2. If we value Soviet quantities produced at US prices, US product appears to be about five times as large as Soviet product. On the other hand, if we value US quantities produced at Soviet prices, the relative superiority of US output appears to be more than five times as great as shown in the first comparison. Which of the two ratios is correct?

TABLE 2

	USSR national product	US national product	Ratio of US to USSR product
At dollar prices	$1,020	$5,000	4.9
At ruble prices	R6,000	R160,000	26.7

First, let us note that the large difference in the two national product ratios is the result of substantial differences in relative prices and relative quantities in the two countries. In our arbitrarily chosen example, guns are five times as expensive as butter in the United States, but cost only half as much as butter in the USSR. To put it another way, the USSR–US price ratio for guns at 5 rubles per dollar is a tenth as large as the price ratio for butter at 50 rubles per dollar. At the same time, the USSR produces half as many guns as the United States but less than 1 per cent as much butter. The divergence of the USSR–US price and quantity ratios is responsible for the divergent values of the ratio of USSR-to-US total product. If, however, the ratio of the USSR price to the US price were the same for all commodities, even though the quantity ratios differed, total product in the USSR would be the same proportion of total product in the United States, whether measured in rubles or dollars.[1]

Obviously, international price ratios are not the same for all commodities—whether the comparison is between the United States and the USSR or any other pair of countries. Within a single economy, the structure of prices changes even over short periods. Can we possibly circumvent the dilemma by avoiding the use of prices or, alternatively, by using the prices of only one economy to measure output in both?

The national product is an aggregate of varying physical quantities of many different goods and services. In order to add dissimilar things, to add guns to butter, we need, in John R. Hicks' phrase, some "rule of equivalence." The particular equivalence rule to be used necessarily depends on our objective in measuring changes or differences in national output. Economists distinguish two broad categories of measurement objectives—changes in productive capacity or in economic welfare, "economic welfare" being defined in terms of the utility of goods to households or to, say, the Central Planning Board, depending on whose preferences shape the allocation of resources in the society.

As it turns out, prices will necessarily be our rule of equivalence for both objectives. For if we are concerned to measure comparative welfare, we require that the quantities of the various goods and services produced be weighted in proportion to their relative utility. If measurement of comparative productive capacity is our objective, commodities must be weighted in proportion to their relative drain on the community's capacity, i.e., in proportion to the relative volume of resources they consume. In either case, as a practical matter, prices are the closest we can come to the equivalences we desire. It is perhaps unnecessary to add that a comparison involving the USSR and the United States will be restricted to measurement of relative capacity, since it is difficult to see what meaning can be attached

1. In our example there is an inverse relationship between price ratios and quantity ratios. Such a relationship is a common characteristic of comparisons involving two economies at a point in time, or the same economy at different points in time. The explanation lies in the tendency for commodities produced on a relatively large scale to be cheaper than those produced on a relatively small scale. But an inverse relationship between price and quantity ratios is not necessary for a divergence in the product ratios. For this, what is necessary is that both the price ratios and the quantity ratios be different for the various products.

to a welfare comparison of two economies which differ radically in the fundamental principle of economic organization—who controls the allocation of resources.

Three important consequences follow from the conclusion that we require price as our equivalence rule. First, any international comparison (analogously, any intertemporal comparison intranationally) will yield two different indexes, corresponding to the two price structures which serve as equivalences, because the structure of relative prices and quantities differs from country to country (and within the same country, from period to period). These differences are inevitable, for they are but the reflections of dissimilar (or changing) structures of preferences and resource availabilities.

Second, neither index is *a priori* preferable over the other. We may add guns and butter and compare US and USSR output using either preference-scarcity pattern as the common measuring rod. However, each pattern is unique, appropriate to only one country. If we wish to compare the respective national outputs of our numerical example in terms of the American pattern, the ratio of total output in the two countries is 4.9. If we ask the distinctly different question of how the national products compare when measured in terms of the Soviet pattern, the answer is 26.7. In each case, the quantities of one country are being valued by alien standards and there is no intrinsic reason to choose one comparison over the other. The correctness of either index depends on the particular resource pattern which is the context of the comparison; neither index is appropriate for both contexts; both indexes are necessary for the complete "truth." [2]

From what has already been said, it should be clear that the average of the two ratios is also not acceptable as the single number characterizing the relation of USSR to US national product. The average reflects neither the dollar nor the ruble price pattern and in principle, therefore, is simply wrong. [3] Use

2. Since there are some important things wrong with Soviet prices as measures of relative opportunity costs, it may be argued that the comparison in ruble prices is misleading. But whatever the inadequacies of Soviet prices, no one would claim that US relative prices are proper indicators of Soviet opportunity costs. Second, it is possible to make certain adjustments in Soviet prices which make them more meaningful for these purposes.

3. That is, there is no economic meaning which can be attached to the average ratio. Attempts have been made to attach such meaning but, to the writer's knowledge, none of these efforts has been successful.

Since it is sometimes claimed that the average, in effect, neutralizes the of the average does less damage when the two ratios are relatively close together (as they are not in the above example). Even so, it is a misleading procedure at best, for the average alone cannot tell us how much the ratios diverge. The average of 4.9 and 26.7 is 15.8. But 15.8 is also the average of 15.7 and 15.9, of 10.0 and 21.6, and of 0.9 (i.e., Soviet product greater than US product) and 30.7, among many others.[4] The larger the spread between the ratios, the less justifiable is the use of the average as their surrogate.

A COMPARISON OF U.S. AND SOVIET GNP

So far, the argument has been based on a hypothetical example. What are the actual numbers? Morris Bornstein, of the University of Michigan, has compared Soviet and US GNP in 1955 for the Joint Economic Committee of the Congress.[5] He estimated total Soviet GNP in 1955 as 26.8 per cent of US GNP in the same year when measured in 1955 ruble prices, and 53.4 per cent when measured in 1955 dollar prices. The geometric average of the two percentages is 37.8. By 1958 Soviet GNP had increased 24 per cent (in real terms) in Bornstein's estimate; US GNP rose by only 2 per cent according to official US figures.

In 1958, then, Soviet GNP can be said to have been about one-third of US GNP, when both are measured in rubles, and about two-thirds as large when measured in dollars. The geometric

---

counteracting biases of the primary ratios, it is necessary to say a word here about the nature of these "biases." Without going into technical detail, suffice it to say that such biases do exist and they result from our unavoidable need to approximate the rates at which resources are mutually substitutable at capacity levels in a wide range of alternative possible output combinations by means of relative prices which refer to only one historical point in that range of combinations. Nevertheless, this does not certify the correctness of the average ratio. In the first place, in this context, the average ratio still has no claim to economic meaning but only to statistical expediency. Second, there is no assurance that the average ratio can fulfill even this limited role of statistical compromise, for we know little about the shape of the curve of alternative output combinations in either economy and, hence, of the direction and magnitude of the biases to which the primary ratios are subject.

4. For statistical reasons, the usual procedure is to employ a geometric rather than arithmetic average. However, the same objection applies to use of either average.

5. "Comparison of Soviet and United States National Product," *Comparisons of the United States and Soviet Economies*, Washington, D.C., 1959, II, p. 385.

average of these ratios is 46 per cent. It is this kind of number—
USSR GNP less than half as large as ours—that is frequently
heard in public discussion.[6] Regrettably, no attempt seems to
have been made to caution the public that this represents an
average of ratios which differ by a factor of two.

Citation of the average ratio without reference to the disparate
components that make it up as misleading because it prevents
recognition of a central fact: Soviet national output is simultaneously considerably smaller than but also almost as large as ours.
Since the context of the public discussion is the Soviet-American
economic race, in which the relative positions of the contestants
at start and "finish" are a prime focus of controversy, use of the
average ratio alone is particularly confusing because it results in
a distorted view of the relative standings at various points in the
future. Thus, according to Allen Dulles,[7] even by 1970 Soviet GNP
will not be much more than 55 per cent of ours. However, using
the same growth rates as underlie the above estimate—4 per cent
for the United States and 6 per cent for the USSR—USSR GNP
in 1965 would be either less than two-fifths or just three-quarters
as large as US GNP, depending on whether the comparison is
based on Soviet or American prices; by 1970 Soviet GNP would be
about 42 per cent or about 82 per cent as large as US GNP. It
goes without saying that the projected relative position of the
USSR is considerably improved in the exercise if the gap between Soviet and US growth rates is increased. If US GNP
increased annually by 3 per cent and Soviet GNP grew by 7
per cent,[8] by 1970 the ruble comparison would show Soviet
GNP somewhat more than half as large; the dollar comparison
would show Soviet GNP *larger* than US GNP.[9] Are we then to be

6. For example, Allen W. Dulles, head of the Central Intelligence Agency,
testified in hearings before the Joint Economic Committee of Congress on
November 13, 1959, that Soviet GNP in 1958 was estimated by CIA as 45
per cent of US GNP in the same year (*Hearings Before the Joint Economic
Committee, 86th Congress, 1st Session, November 13–20, 1959*, Washington, D.C., 1960, p. 4). I want to point out that Professor Bornstein's understanding and treatment of the index-number problem in Soviet-American
comparisons are above reproach. I have used his estimates as the basis of
the discussion, not as an example of the practices I am criticizing.

7. *Ibid.*, p. 9.

8. Three per cent is the approximate US average rate of growth over the
past half-century, as well as of the last nine years; 7 per cent is CIA's estimate, according to Mr. Dulles, of the Soviet growth rate for 1950–1958.

9. The Soviet claim is that the national income of the USSR is now
about 60 per cent as large as ours, both defined according to the Marxist

alarmed by the dollar comparisons or comforted by the ruble
ratios?

One more statistical rabbit remains to be pulled out of the hat.
The above projections are based on 1955 ruble and dollar price
patterns. Should the price trends of the past decade be maintained in the next—i.e., if the Soviet Union should succeed in
maintaining price stability or even moderate deflation, and if the
US economy should continue to suffer from appreciable price
inflation—Soviet GNP might well "overtake and surpass" US
GNP, both measured in dollar prices of the *given year,* considerably before 1970. At the same time, the gap between ruble-based
and dollar-based GNP ratios would have diminished appreciably,
and even when valued in ruble prices (again, of the given year),
Soviet GNP would appear respectably close in over-all size to
US GNP.

At this point, the observer on the sidelines is within his rights
in asking whether the game is worth the candle. Are we in effect
engaging in "some meaningless parlor game devised in the Krem-
lin"? [10] Yet, it is important to bring home to the public a point
which, though seemingly obvious, encounters considerable emo-
tional resistance: if the Soviet economy continues to grow faster
than ours, at some point in the future it will inevitably be larger
than ours. A passage from a paper prepared for the Congressional Joint Economic Committee illustrates an attitude still
widely held in this country: "The realistic expectation as of the
present time is that our relative advantage over the Russians will
diminish but at a slackening rate. . . . There is no sufficient reason to feel sure that she [USSR] cannot some day match us in
per capita output, although most of us may properly have sufficient confidence in the superiority of our own system to doubt
that she can do so." [11]

---

concept, and that growth rates of 8 per cent for the USSR and 2 to 3
per cent for the United States mark the crossover dates as 1968 for total
output and 1970 for per capita output. (Index-number problems rarely
intrude on Soviet-made projections.) See, for example, A. Aganbegian,
"Dognat' i peregnat' SShA po urovniu proizvoditelnosti truda" [Overtake
and surpass the USA with respect to the level of productivity of labor],
Sotsialisticheskii trud, No. 4 (1959), p. 22.

10. Hans Heymann, Jr., "Problems of Soviet–United States Comparisons,"
Comparisons of the United States and Soviet Economies, I, p. 10.

11. Howard C. Peterson (Committee on Economic Development), "Soviet Economic Growth and United States Policy," *ibid.,* II, p. 519.

Beyond this limited educational goal, however, comparisons of total GNP alone are not useful measures of the course of the Soviet-American economic race. We have seen that such comparisons are highly sensitive to the price patterns which are the means by which different quantities of dissimilar products are made commensurable. Whether we use dollar prices or ruble prices, whether prices of 1955 or 1965, makes an enormous difference to the results, each of which is equally "true" within its own defined context. Moreover, the baskets of goods being compared are so radically different in their composition that any measuring procedure attempting to make the baskets comparable does violence to the reality.

Fortunately, it is *not* the over-all size of the baskets but what is in them that is of direct interest to us. The central issues of public policy posed by the speed of Soviet growth hinge on the fear that rapid economic progress enhances Soviet ability to carry out its hostile designs against the free world; and here the over-all GNP comparison supplies only the truism that a large and fast-growing GNP does signify an expanding resource base for the execution of Soviet policy. In contrast, comparisons of defense efforts, levels of consumption, foreign aid programs— in the context of the total quantity of resources available to each country—are the direct approaches to effective policy decisions. Fortunately, too, though unduly burdened with the relatively sterile over-all GNP comparisons, public American discussion has recognized the need to focus on the specific components of total output relevant to the issue at hand.

MILITARY EXPENDITURES AND THEIR BURDEN

Since the truly critical issue is relative military capabilities, major attention has been devoted to comparisons of the size of Soviet and American military budgets. The prevalent estimate seems to be that, with Soviet output not yet half as large as ours, the Soviet military budget "in real terms" is about as large as ours.[12] Obviously, this implies that the share of GNP devoted to military uses is twice as large in the USSR as in the United States. In some estimates, the Soviet relative effort is even

12. [The value of Soviet defense expenditures in U.S. prices was $40 billion, about the same as U.S. national security outlays in the same year. *Editor.*]

larger: according to Adlai Stevenson, "It is said that the Soviet defense effort takes about 25 per cent of the national income as against 10 per cent in this country." [13]

For all its apparent internal consistency, this set of relations is just poor arithmetic. I have already noted that to obtain an over-all GNP ratio of around 1:2 requires the averaging of separate comparisons in dollars and rubles. Assuming that the other relations cited are also derived from an account representing the geometric average of separate ruble and dollar comparisons, suppose we convert geometric average comparisons of defense and total GNP into absolute dollar comparisons. The results are shown in Table 3, using Bornstein's data for 1955 for illustration.

TABLE 3

	US billion $ (1)	Geometric average ratio, USSR to US (2)	USSR billion $ (2) x (1) (3)
Defense	38.4	.843	32.4
GNP	397.5	.378	150.3

Taking the US dollar values and multiplying them by USSR-to-US geometric average ratios, we obtain column (3), USSR values in dollars. Defense accounts for 10 per cent of US GNP of $397.5 billion, but 22 per cent of the Soviet GNP of $150.3 billion. It is in these terms that it appears the USSR is devoting more than twice as much of its national product to defense as does the United States. However, if we attempt the same procedure for all components of GNP, we will encounter an embarrassing discrepancy between the sum of USSR GNP components converted in this fashion and the converted value of *total* GNP, as shown in Table 4. The sum of column (3) elements in this table is 172.2; but 37.8 per cent of 397.5 is 150.3. The impasse is clear.

Thus, it is entirely improper to compare US and USSR shares of GNP allocated for component uses when the USSR elements in the comparison represent an average percentage of corresponding US values. Once more the average of separate ruble and dollar comparisons has proved an unreliable guide, this time

13. "Putting First Things First," *Foreign Affairs*, xxxviii, No. 2 (January 1960), p. 200.

TABLE 4

	US billion $ (1)	Geometric average ratio, USSR to US (2)	USSR billion $ (2) x (1) (3)
Consumption	269.7	.285	76.9
Investment	77.2	.577	44.5
Defense	38.4	.843	32.4
Administration	12.1	1.523	18.4
GNP	397.5 *	.378	?

* Slight discrepancy between total and sum of components due to rounding.

leading into an arithmetic dead-end.

On occasion it appears that the arithmetic fallacies of such a procedure are at least dimly perceived, though loyalty to the average ratio for total GNP is unwavering. The resulting need to avoid the arithmetic impasse just described can lead to an economic defense which is dangerously misleading. A case in point is an Intelligence Information Brief of the State Department's Office of Intelligence Research and Analysis, entitled "US Versus Soviet Spending for Major GNP Categories" (February 24, 1959). After estimating the value of Soviet defense expenditures in 1957 in US prices as $40 billion, or about the same as US national security outlays, the document continues: "While the cost of the Soviet defense apparatus is 40 billion dollars, it would be a mistake to conclude that the USSR devotes 23 percent of its GNP of about 175 billion dollars (at 1957 US prices) to defense for it obtains at a lower cost what in American prices is worth 40 billion dollars. The Soviet armament industry is the most efficient among Soviet industries, and Soviet soldiers live more modestly than US soldiers. In other words, the Soviet military establishment requires fewer resources to produce the same destructive power as its American counterpart. While the Soviet national product is only 40 percent as large as that of the US (440 billion dollars), the share of defense in the totals is not much higher in the USSR than in the US."

From what has been said previously, it is evident that the State Department's estimate of USSR GNP in 1957 as 40 per cent of ours is also the average of separate ruble and dollar comparisons of total GNP. The new element here is the explicit step of taking 40 per cent of US GNP, obtaining a sum of 175 billion dollars, and calling that sum Soviet GNP at 1957 US prices. Of course, it is nothing of the sort. The process of obtaining the average of ruble and dollar comparisons means that the prices in which Soviet quantities are being valued are neither dollar nor ruble but "something in between." Since there exists no economy with a set of relative prices corresponding to "something in between" US and Soviet prices, the estimate of Soviet GNP as 175 billion dollars should be expressed in an equally imaginary currency unit. Certainly, the latter has no business masquerading as a dollar.

The authors of the Brief are aware that "it would be a mistake to conclude that the USSR devotes 23 percent of its GNP of about 175 billion dollars . . . to defense." However, they apparently fail to recognize the true reason—the incompatibility of their USSR GNP figure, derived from US GNP in dollars, by applying an average USSR-to-US-GNP ratio, and the estimate of Soviet defense outlays, obtained by dollar-price valuation of Soviet quantities. Instead, the authors attempt to resolve the dilemma by reference to differences in the efficiency of resource utilization.

If the Soviet defense package costs 40 billion dollars in American prices, what does it mean to say that the package was obtained at a lower cost? Less in terms of rubles? Ambiguity here is the result of a basic misunderstanding of the meaning of the values compared. Contrary to what is clearly asserted in the quoted passage, it is not true that equivalent volumes of destructive power are being compared.[14] Since the Soviet defense package differs significantly from the US defense package in the amounts and proportions allocated to personnel, hardware, and so forth, the identity of the dollar-value tags on the two packages tells us only that, when resources are valued as in the United States, the two packages represent equivalent volumes of resources used. The structure of resource use will, of course, be different for the two packages. With no other information provided, we know nothing of the comparative destructive power of the Soviet and US defense expenditures. If personnel are expensive in dollars but cheap in rubles, and if hardware is, conversely, expensive in rubles but cheap in dollars, valuing US and Soviet defense expenditures in rubles is likely to show US out-

14. This point is explicitly recognized at an earlier point in the Brief, only to be ignored in the passage under discussion.

lays perceptibly larger than Soviet outlays because of relatively heavier emphasis on ruble-expensive hardware in the US program than in the Soviet program. If this is the case, the ruble comparison would indicate that, when resources are valued as in the USSR, the US defense package is a heavier *absolute* resource drain than the Soviet. Again, destructive power is neither relevant to nor implied in this comparison.

It is clear that comparisons of structure and components of GNP in the two countries must be framed in a consistent set of accounts—dollar or ruble, but not a mixture of both. It is equally clear, however, that we shall again be faced with a substantial divergence in the results. If Soviet GNP, in dollar terms, is *not* less than half but almost two-thirds as large as ours, near-identity of the absolute outlays in defense (when measured in dollars) must mean that the *relative* burden is not much more than 50 per cent larger in the USSR than in the United States, rather than twice as large, as is commonly believed. On the other hand, a switch to ruble valuation would show that Soviet defense outlays were three times as large a *relative* burden as American defense expenditures.

To express the purpose of the comparison as an attempt to compare the relative burden of defense outlays in the two countries suggests, however, that valuing both GNP's in dollars or rubles is begging the question. If relative prices in the USSR were the same as in the United States, the economic burden of Soviet defense expenditures, defined in terms of the share of GNP, would be measured by a dollar valuation. But relative prices are not the same, and we could certainly balk at measuring the burden of US defense outlays in terms of ruble relative prices.[15] It would seem sensible to measure the relative burden of expenditures in each country in terms of its own price pattern —its own scheme of scarcities and preferences.

A reliable source reports seeing a desk sign in the Pentagon warning the staff, "The boss wants a single figure—not a range." Yet despite the policymaker's expressed indignation at the technician's propensity to statistical hedging, the researcher has been able to make his boss understand about such things as the un-

15. Bornstein estimates that, in ruble prices, defense consumed only 4 per cent of the US GNP in 1955. Advocates of larger US defense budgets might be interested in this comparison for public relations purposes.

reliability of data and the uncertainties of forecasting. On the other hand, up to now it has been assumed that, to the uninitiated, the index-number problem must appear abstruse and the concept of two complementary ratios which do not embrace a range as positively occult.

But the game of US–USSR comparisons is too important to be played other than by the rule-book. Is it not time to cease treating the index-number problem as an esoteric possession of the academics, too difficult for the public to comprehend?

Toward that end, we may summarize some of the important rules of the game:

(1) Because of significant differences in the economic structure of the USSR and the United States, comparison of national output or its components must yield divergent measures of the ratio of absolute values. There exists no unique answer. The divergent measures are each equally "true."

(2) The average of the divergent ratios has no intrinsic meaning, and its use as a shorthand summary in lieu of the real ratios is defensible only when the divergence is relatively small, as it is not in the case of US–USSR comparisons.

(3) Apart from the fact of large divergence of the real ratios, the average ratio may not be used to develop absolute USSR values from corresponding US dollar values, especially for structural comparisons.

(4) Although not a clear violation, in the interests of more sensible determination of the score, the practice of measuring the relative burden of Soviet expenditures on components of GNP in terms of dollars might be forsworn. Efforts are burdensome in terms of one's own system of values, not the other fellow's.

For the sake of public understanding of some of the vital issues of our time, it is urgent that we resume playing by the rules.

The Soviet Twenty-year Program

This is an excerpt from the draft program of Soviet economic policy over the next twenty years presented by Chairman Nikita S. Khrushchev to the Twenty-second Congress of the Soviet Communist Party held in August, 1961.

THE OCTOBER REVOLUTION led the country on to the road of socialism. The path which the Soviet people were to traverse was an unexplored and arduous one. The reactionary forces of the old world did all they could to strangle the Soviet state at its birth. The young Soviet Republic had to cope with intervention and civil war, economic blockade and disruption, conspiracies, sabotage, subversion, terrorism and numerous other trials. Socialist construction was rendered incredibly difficult by the socioeconomic, technical and cultural backwardness of the country.

The point at issue at the time was: either perish or forge full steam ahead and overtake the capitalist countries economically.

The Soviet state had first of all to solve the problem of industrialization. In a historically brief period, without outside help, the Soviet Union built up a large-scale modern industry. By the time it had fulfilled three five-year plans (1928–1941) the Soviet Union had become a mighty industrial power that had achieved complete economic independence from the capitalist countries. Its defense capacity had increased immeasurably. The industrialization of the U.S.S.R. was a great exploit performed by the working class and the people as a whole, for they spared no effort or means, and consciously made sacrifices to lift the country out of its backward state.

Crisis of World Capitalism · World War I and the October Revolution ushered in the general crisis of capitalism. The second stage of this crisis developed at the time of World War II and the Socialist revolutions in a number of European and Asian countries. World capitalism has now entered a new, third stage of that crisis, the principal feature of which is that its develop-

57

ment was not due to a world war.

The breakaway from capitalism of more and more countries; the weakening of imperialist positions in the economic competition with socialism; the breakup of the imperialist colonial system; the intensification of imperialist contradictions with the development of state-monopoly capitalism and the growth of militarism; the mounting internal instability and decay of capitalist economy evidenced by the increasing inability of capitalism to make full use of the productive forces (low rates of production growth, periodic crises, continuous underloading of production plant, and chronic unemployment); the mounting struggle between labor and capital; an acute intensification of contradictions within the world capitalist economy; and unprecedented growth of political reaction in all spheres, rejection of bourgeois freedom and establishment of Fascist and despotic regimes in a number of countries, and the profound crisis of bourgeois policy and ideology—all these are manifestations of the general crisis of capitalism.

In the imperialist stage state-monopoly capitalism comes to the fore. The emergence and growth of monopolies leads to the direct intervention of the state, in the interests of the financial oligarchy, in the process of capitalist reproduction.

Theories Laid in the Dust · Attempts at state regulation of the capitalist economy cannot eliminate competition and anarchy of production, cannot insure the planned development of the economy on a nationwide scale because capitalist ownership and exploitation of wage-labor remain the basis of production. The bourgeois theories of "crisis-free" and "planned" capitalism have been laid in the dust by the development of contemporary capitalist economy.

The new phenomena in imperialist development corroborate the accuracy of Lenin's conclusions on the principal objective laws of capitalism in its final stage and on its increasing decay. Yet this decay does not signify complete stagnation, a palsy of its productive forces, and does not rule out growth of capitalist economy at particular times and in particular countries.

All in all, capitalism is increasingly impeding the development of the contemporary productive forces. Mankind is entering the period of a great scientific and technical revolution bound up with the conquest of nuclear energy, space exploration, the development of chemistry, automation and other major achievements of science and engineering. But the relations of production under capitalism are much too narrow for a scientific and technical revolution. Socialism alone is capable of effecting it and of applying its fruits in the interests of society.

THE TASKS OF THE COMMUNIST PARTY

The C.P.S.U., being a party of scientific communism, proposes and fulfills the task of Communist construction in step with the preparation and maturing of the material and spiritual prerequisites, considering that it would be wrong to jump over necessary stages of development and that it would be equally wrong to halt at an achieved level and thus check progress. The building of communism must be carried out by successive stages.

In the current decade (1961–1970), the Soviet Union, in creating the material and technical basis of communism, will surpass the strongest and richest capitalist country, the U.S.A., in production per head of population; the people's standard of living and their cultural and technical standards will improve substantially; everyone will live in easy circumstances; all collective and state farms will become highly productive and profitable enterprises; the demand of the Soviet people for well-appointed housing will, in the main, be satisfied; hard physical work will disappear; the U.S.S.R. will become the country with the shortest working day.

In the next decade (1971–1980) the material and technical basis of communism will be created and there will be an abundance of material and cultural benefits for the whole population. Soviet society will come close to a stage where it can introduce the principle of distribution according to needs, and there will be a gradual transition to one form of ownership—public ownership. Thus, a Communist society will, on the whole, be built in the U.S.S.R. The construction of Communist society will be fully completed in the subsequent period.

The majestic edifice of communism is being erected by the persevering effort of the Soviet people—the working class, the peasantry and the intelligentsia. The more successful their work, the closer the great goal—Communist society.

Promotion of the Material and Technical Basis of Communism · In contrast to capitalism, the planned Socialist system of economy combines accelerated technical progress with the full employment of all able-bodied citizens. Automation and comprehensive mechanization serve as a material basis for the gradual development of Socialist labor into Communist labor. Technical progress will require higher standards of production and a higher level of the vocational and general education of all workers. The new machinery developed will be used to improve radically the Soviet people's working conditions, and make them easier, to reduce the length of the working day, to improve living conditions, eliminate hard physical work and subsequently, all unskilled labor.

The creation of the material and technical basis of communism will call for huge investments. The task is to utilize these investments most rationally and economically, with the maximum effect and gain of time.

With these aims in view, the C.P.S.U. plans the following increases in total industrial output:

Within the current ten years, by approximately 150 per cent, exceeding the contemporary level of U.S. industrial output.

Within twenty years, by not less than 500 per cent, leaving the present over-all volume of U.S. industrial output far behind.

Productivity Increase Needed · To achieve this, it is necessary to raise productivity of labor in industry by more than 100 per cent within ten years, and by 300 to 350 per cent within twenty years. In twenty years' time labor productivity in Soviet industry will exceed the present level of labor productivity in the U.S.A. by roughly 100 per cent, and considerably more in terms of per-hour output, due to the reduction of the working day in the U.S.S.R.

Living Standards of the People · The heroic labor of the Soviet people has produced a powerful and versatile economy. There is now every possibility to improve rapidly the living standards of the entire population—the workers, peasants, and intellectuals. The C.P.S.U. sets the historically important task of achieving in the Soviet Union a living standard higher than that of any of the capitalist countries.

This task will be effected by: (A) Raising the individual payment of employees according to the quantity and quality of work, coupled with reduction of retail prices and abolition of taxes paid by the population, (B) Increase of the public funds distributed among members of society irrespective of quantity and quality of their labor, that is, free of charge (education, medical treatment, pensions, maintenance of children at children's institutions, transition to cost-free use of public amenities, etc.).

The rise of the real incomes of the population will be outstripped by rapid increase in the amount of commodities and services, and far-flung construction of dwellings and cultural and service buildings.

Soviet people will be more prosperous than people in the developed capitalist countries even if average incomes will be equal, because in the Soviet Union the national income is distributed fairly among the members of society and there are no parasitical classes as in the bourgeois countries who appropriate and squander immense wealth plundered from millions of working people.

Provision of a High Level of Income and Consumption for the Whole Population · The national income of the U.S.S.R. in the next ten years will increase nearly 150 per cent, and about 400 per cent in twenty years. The real income per head of population will increase by more than 250 per cent in twenty years.

As the incomes of the population grow, the general level of popular consumption will rise rapidly.

Output of consumer goods must meet the growing consumer demand in full, and must conform to its changes. Timely output of goods in accordance with the varied demand of the population, with consideration for local, national and climatic conditions, is an imperative requirement for the consumer industries. Good shopping facilities will be arranged throughout the country, this being a necessary and important condition for the satisfaction of the growing requirements of the population.

The second decade will see an abundance of material and cultural benefits for the whole population, and material prerequisites will be created to complete the transition to the Communist principle of distribution according to need in the period to follow.

The U.S. Target in the Current Decade

THE COUNCIL OF ECONOMIC ADVISERS

In the Employment Act of 1946 the Congress authorized the President to establish a Council to advise the government on economic policy and to report to the President on the conditions and prospects of the nation's economy. This statement is part of the Council's 1962 Annual Report; it was echoed in President Kennedy's Economic Message to the Congress in the same year.

GOALS, IF they are to be useful, should be neither too easy nor too difficult. To set a goal that would have been achieved anyway serves no useful purpose. To set a goal that is obviously impossible of achievement invites a loss of confidence and perhaps failure to achieve what is possible. A good target is one that can be met, but not without effort.

This general limitation sets only a range of growth targets for the United States in the 1960's. It is no easy matter to say exactly how fast an economy can grow, or to obtain consensus on how fast it should grow. Some of the benefits of growth have already been discussed. The costs of growth are the diversion of resources from the satisfaction of current needs to those uses which will yield increased output in the future, and the strain on our institutions and social fabric which this diversion might entail. Ultimately, a democratic society achieves one rate of growth rather than another through the freely made economic and political decisions of its citizens. The task of economic analysis is to show what the choices are, what alternative choices will cost, and what benefits they may yield.

The basic determinants of a society's productive capacity in any year are as follows:

(1) The number of people available for employment, the number of hours they wish to work, their incentives and motivations, and their health, general education, occupational desires, and vocational skills;

(2) The stock of new and old plant and equipment, and its

composition by age, type, and location;

(3) The terms on which the economy has access to natural resources, whether through domestic production or imports;

(4) The level of technology, covering the range from managerial and organizational competence to scientific, engineering, and mechanical understanding;

(5) The efficiency with which resources, domestic and foreign, are allocated to different economic ends, and the extent of monopolistic or other barriers to the movement of labor and capital from low-productivity to high-productivity uses.

These basic determinants interact in complex ways. For example, advanced machinery is of little use without skilled labor to operate it; advanced technology often requires capital equipment to embody it.

Next year's productive capacity will exceed this year's to the extent that the basic determinants can be expanded and improved. Success in achieving a higher rate of growth in the future depends on our willingness to spend current resources to expand our production potential and by our skill and luck in spending them effectively.

The record of economic growth in the United States does not suggest that the average growth rate realized in the past is an immutable natural constant, leaving no scope for growth-stimulating policies. The rate of growth of output has varied from one span of years to another, depending on specific economic circumstances. There was one prolonged period of stagnation—the decade of the 1930's—when potential output grew at less than the average long-term rate, and realized output grew more slowly still. Again, there have been periods when potential output expanded more rapidly than the past average. The postwar years have been such a period of accelerated growth.

Table 1 shows, for the 1947–60 period, the increases in realized and potential GNP, population, labor force, employment, manhours, GNP per person, and productivity. Approximately four-fifths of the annual increase in potential GNP during the period is explained by increases in output per man-hour and one-fifth by increases in total man-hours worked. The increase in output per man-hour is, of course, the resultant of improvements in the quality of the labor force, the quantity and quality of capital, the level of technology, and still other factors.

But consideration of the years 1947–60 as a unit masks signifi-

TABLE 1.—*Output, Population, Labor Input, and Productivity, 1947–60*

Item	Unit	1947	1954	1960[1]	Percentage change per year		
					1947–54	1954–60	1947–60
Output:							
Gross national product	Billions of dollars	324.9	422.0	511.1	3.8	3.2	3.5
Potential GNP[2]	Billions of dollars	324.9	440.5	541.8	4.4	3.5	4.0
Population	Millions of persons	144.1	162.4	180.7	1.7	1.8	1.8
Labor input:							
Labor force[3]	Millions of persons	61.8	67.8	73.1	1.3	1.3	1.3
Employment[3]	Millions of persons	59.4	64.2	69.2	1.1	1.3	1.2
Potential empl.[4]	Millions of persons	59.4	65.1	70.2	1.3	1.3	1.3
Man-hours	Billions of man-hours	129.6	132.9	139.7	.4	.8	.6
Potential man-hours[5]	Billions of man-hours	129.6	135.4	143.1	.6	.9	.8
GNP per capita	Dollars	2,255	2,599	2,828	2.0	1.4	1.8
Productivity:							
GNP per worker	Dollars	5,470	6,573	7,386	2.7	2.0	2.3
Potential GNP per worker	Dollars	5,470	6,768	7,718	3.1	2.2	2.7
GNP per man-hour	Dollars	2.51	3.18	3.66	3.4	2.4	2.9
Potential GNP per man-hour	Dollars	2.51	3.25	3.79	3.8	2.6	3.2

1. Data include Alaska and Hawaii. 2. Same as actual in 1947; in 1954 and 1960, calculated from 3.5 percent trend line through mid-1955. 3. Includes armed forces. 4. Assumes 4 percent unemployment rate for all periods, with no adjustment for cyclical movement of the labor force. 5. Same as actual in 1947; in 1954 and 1960, assumes 4 percent unemployment rate and corrects for decline in hours induced by recession. *Note.*—Dollars in 1961 prices.
sources: Department of Commerce, Department of Labor, and Council of Economic Advisers.

cant differences within the period. There was a substantial slowing down in the growth of potential output between the first and
the second part of this period. From 1947 to 1954, potential GNP
grew at a rate of 4.4 percent a year, and from 1954 to 1960 at a
rate of 3.5 percent. Since the labor force grew at a rate of 1.3
percent a year in both periods and average hours worked fell
somewhat more slowly after 1954 than before, the slower rate
of growth that has taken place since 1954 is explained by a decline in the rate of increase of productivity. This decline resulted
in part from a more slowly rising trend of productivity within
nonmanufacturing industry, and in part from a shift—usual in
slack periods—from manufacturing to nonmanufacturing in the
composition of economic activity.

TABLE 2.—*Growth of Gross National Product per Man-Year,
Selected Countries, 1913–59*

[Percent per year]

Country	1913–59	1950–59
Japan	2.6	6.1
Italy	1.7	4.7
Germany	1.4	4.5
France	1.5	3.6
Netherlands	1.3	3.4
Norway	1.9	3.1
Sweden	1.7	2.8
United States	1.8	2.2
Canada	1.5	2.0
Denmark	1.2	1.8
United Kingdom	.8	1.7

Note.—Gross national product at constant prices was used wherever
available. See *National Institute Economic Review*, No. 16, July 1961, pp.
36 and 46–47, for data and description of sources of materials used.

SOURCE: National Institute of Economic and Social Research.

Further evidence that modern industrial economies are not
helpless prisoners of past long-term trends is to be found in Table
2,[1] which shows that the major countries of Western Europe, and
Japan as well, have recently exceeded their own long-term per-
formances.

1. [This table and other data relating to the long-term growth of the
industrial nations are the subject of the article which follows by D. C. Paige
and others of the National Institute of Economic and Social Research.
Editor.]

On June 28, President Kennedy stated that a growth rate of 4.5 percent yearly is "well within our capability." On November 17, the United States joined with the other 19 member nations of the Organization for Economic Cooperation and Development in setting as a target the attainment of a 50 percent (4.1 percent a year) increase in their combined national product during the decade from 1960 to 1970. The ability of the United States to meet, and even to exceed, this target is the best guarantee of success for the OECD. A high rate of growth of potential output will not be reached immediately. The policies to achieve it, even if adopted now, will not bear fruit at once, and it will not be achieved without effort. But in the second half of the decade, with the help of a rapidly growing labor force, it should be possible to exceed a growth rate of 4.5 percent annually and to achieve an average rate of growth of potential output of 4.3 percent between 1960 and 1970.

If this growth is achieved and if, in addition, 1970 is a year of 4 percent unemployment, actual GNP will grow at an average annual rate of 4.9 percent (Table 3). The difference between this figure and 4.3 percent reflects the current shortfall of actual output from potential output. Such a rate of growth of total GNP would mean an annual increase of GNP per person in the population of 3.2 percent, nearly double the rate achieved during the 1947–60 period. It is this figure which most nearly measures the gain to society from accelerated economic growth. If, by 1970, we succeed in achieving an unemployment rate below 4 percent, even further increases in output will become possible. To a first approximation, each 1 point decline in the 1970 unemployment rate would add about $8 billion to 1970 GNP and about 0.1 to the annual rate of growth.

Table 3 is in no sense a prediction of what will actually occur. It shows what would be required to move up to and beyond a 4.5 percent growth rate, giving us a rate of growth of potential for the full decade averaging 4.3 percent a year. Demographic factors lay the foundation for a significant acceleration of potential output. If labor force projections are realized and if past trends in hours worked per man year continue, available labor input will increase during the 1960's at more than one and one-

TABLE 3.—*Output, Population, Labor Input, and Productivity, 1960 Actual and 1970 Illustrative*

Item	Unit	1960 [1]	1970 illustrative [2]	Percentage change per year 1960–70
Output:				
Gross national product	Billions of dollars	511.1	825	4.9
Potential gross national product	Billions of dollars	541.8	825	4.3
Population	Millions of persons	180.7	213.8	1.7
Labor input:				
Labor force [3]	Millions of persons	73.1	87.1	1.8
Employment [3]	Millions of persons	69.2	83.7	1.9
Potential employment	Millions of persons	70.2	83.7	1.8
Man-hours	Billions of man-hours	139.7	162	1.5
Potential man-hours	Billions of man-hours	143.1	162	1.2
GNP per capita	Dollars	2,828	3,858	3.2
Productivity:				
GNP per worker	Dollars	7,386	9,868	2.9
Potential GNP per worker	Dollars	7,718	9,868	2.5
GNP per man-hour	Dollars	3.66	5.09	3.4
Potential GNP per man-hour	Dollars	3.79	5.09	3.0

1. Potential series for 1960 based on the following assumptions: *GNP*, calculated from 3.5 percent trend line through mid-1955; *employment*, 4 percent unemployment rate; *man-hours*, 4 percent unemployment rate and correction for decline in hours induced by recession.

2. Illustrative figures for 1970 based on the following assumptions: *Potential GNP growth* rate of 4.3 percent per year from 1960 to 1970, with actual and potential being the same in 1970; *population*, 1955–57 fertility levels continue to 1980; *labor force*, participation rate of 57.8 percent of non-institutional population 14 years of age and over; *employment*, 4 percent unemployment rate; *man-hours*, continuation of previous trend.

3. Includes armed forces.

Note.—Data includes Alaska and Hawaii. Dollars in 1961 prices.

SOURCES: Department of Commerce, Department of Labor, and Council of Economic Advisers.

half times its rate of growth during the 1947–60 period. With this increase in labor input, it is a matter of arithmetic that a 3 percent yearly increase in man-hour productivity would be needed if the annual rate of growth of potential GNP is to average 4.3 percent over the decade.

The required growth of output per man-hour was surpassed in the 1947–54 period, but since 1954 performance has fallen below what is required. The vigorous growth of the early postwar period benefited from the possibility of renewing a capital stock which had aged during the depression and war years of low investment. Making good this backlog of investment demand brought with it the quick realization of latent technological progress. Simple continuation of recent trends will not be sufficient to repeat that performance.

The population upsurge which began in the 1940's, together with the expected decline in death rates, will give us a rapid increase in the population of working age. Adult women are expected to enter the labor force in increasing proportions; but because a larger fraction of our youth will remain in school and because the trend toward earlier retirement among male workers is likely to continue, over-all labor force participation rates are expected to remain steady. The resultant of these factors should be a labor force in 1970 of a little more than 87 million, an annual rate of increase of 1.8 percent in this decade, compared with the distinctly lower rate of 1.3 percent from 1947 to 1960. If 4 percent of the labor force is unemployed in 1970, total employment will come to 83.7 million. A reduction in the unemployment rate to 3 percent would add over 800,000 to employment.

These beneficial effects of labor force growth will not occur automatically. New efforts in education, technological development, capital formation, and other areas will be required. In particular, unless technical progress brings an unexpected increase in the productivity of capital, a major rise in capital investment will be needed.

Economic Growth: The Last Hundred Years

DEBORAH C. PAIGE WITH F. T. BLACKABY AND

S. FREUND

Deborah C. Paige and her colleagues are staff economists at the National Institute of Economic and Social Research. The National Institute is supported by British firms to conduct economic research into business conditions and public policy in the United Kingdom. This article first appeared in the July 1961 Economic Review *published by the Institute.*

INTRODUCTION

Since the war the economies of some developed countries appear to have been growing exceptionally fast (Table 1). From

TABLE 1. *Recent and Long-Term Growth Rates in National Product per Man-Year*

Annual per cent increases

	Long-term rate		1950–1959	1954–1959
	Starting year	Rate		
Japan	*1880*	2.9	6.1	7.6
Italy	*1863*	1.2	4.7	3.8
Germany	*1853*	1.5	4.5	3.6
France	*1855*	1.5	3.6	3.3
Netherlands	*1900*	1.1	3.4	2.9
Norway	*1865*	1.6	3.1	2.5
Sweden	*1863*	2.1	2.8	3.0
United States	*1871*	2.0	2.2	2.2
Canada	*1872*	1.7	2.0	1.8
Denmark	*1872*	1.6	1.8	2.5
United Kingdom	*1857*	1.2	1.7	1.6

1950 onwards six countries have shown growth rates of 3 to 6 per cent; four of these have shown rates of over 3 per cent since 1954, by which time the effects of post-war recovery might be expected to have been over. These rates are nearly all more than twice as high as the long-term averages of the countries concerned. Does this imply that they are some kind of spurt rates which will inevitably revert, sooner or later, to more 'normal' rates of growth?

This is one of the questions raised by a study of long-term growth rates; it leads on to others. Is there any sense in the concept of a normal rate of growth—either a general normal rate for all industrial countries or a specific normal rate for individual ones? Do the same countries show rapid rates of growth over long periods? Do all countries show rapid rates at certain stages of development? Are fast rates linked to population increases?

The amount of information available about growth rates in the last 50–100 years has increased considerably during recent years. This article collects the figures together, appraises them, and attempts to show what conclusions can and cannot be drawn from them. The countries studied include all the eight Western European nations for which adequate long-term series could be found, as well as the United States, Canada and Japan. No attempt has been made to include countries of the Eastern bloc; the problems of the measurement and comparability of their figures are a separate subject.

THE FIGURES

In most economic articles, any assessment of the figures can quite properly be relegated to a statistical appendix; but in a discussion of the rates of economic growth over a century the first question that springs to mind is whether the figures are sufficiently reliable and meaningful for any useful conclusions to be drawn. This must be discussed, at least in broad terms, before any comparisons are made.

In this article, the measure of growth used is the rate of increase in real national product per head of the employed labour force. For most countries, official currently-constructed national product series have only been in existence since the second world war, and estimates for the earlier period have been calculated retrospectively. These retrospective estimates depend on fewer series and have a larger margin of error than post-war figures; but the estimates in current prices appear moderately reliable over quite long periods. A much larger margin of error enters in when they are adjusted for price changes—as they must be before growth can be measured in real terms.

Even if full information were available, it would not be possible to construct one definitive series of national product estimates in constant prices; there is an inherent 'index number problem' that cannot be avoided. There is no unique measure of changes in prices: when the price movements of different goods diverge, the index obtained depends upon the year whose pattern of expenditure is used to provide the weights. In short periods, and periods when most prices move together, different weighting patterns produce fairly similar results. But the price indices linking pre- and post-war years, or spanning periods of rapid technological change, are likely to vary considerably according to the base year taken.

Tentative and indirect evidence suggests that a change from a series corrected by detailed price indices using initial year weights to one corrected by price indices using end-year weights might change the growth rate by 50 per cent or more over a period of, say, thirty years, including a major war. Such differences are seldom found in practice because the series used are usually amalgams of differently-weighted component series, which can only be regarded as a rather inaccurate approximation to the mean of the two extremes.

For earlier periods these index number difficulties are outweighed by the problem of finding any price index which is at all appropriate. Usually the choice is between a wholesale price index and a cost-of-living index based on working-class expenditure patterns. Neither of them is really suitable for adjusting national income figures. The wholesale price indices tend to be little more than indices of primary product prices. The cost-of-living indices give a large weight to food and rent, and only a small weight to manufactured goods. Both indices may therefore overstate the price rise for the national product as a whole, since in parts of the nineteenth century the relative prices of manufactured goods fell sharply.

Growth rates also need to be adjusted for population changes, and preferably for employment changes. (Ideally, they should be adjusted for hours of work, which fell considerably in the earlier period; but there is not enough information to make com-

plete estimates of average hours worked.) For many countries
the employment series before 1938 are not satisfactory. Most of
the estimates used in the inter-war period were obtained by cal-
culating participation rates from the census years, applying these
rates to population estimates for the years between the censuses,
and then adjusting these figures by annual estimates of unemployment. For some countries these unemployment figures are
based on trade union returns, and may therefore show too great
a cyclical fluctuation; thus some of the apparent fluctuations in
output per man in Norway and Sweden may not be real.

Before 1913, since labour force estimates for many countries
are unreliable, the increase in national product was divided by
the increase in population of working age. These figures are a
rather poor substitute for labour force figures; but where separate
labour force estimates exist, the average rate of increase in the
population of working age was not very different from that in
the labour force in the period up to 1913.

Assessment · The margin of error in the figures, therefore, is a
wide one; and the further back the figures go, the wider the
margin is. An estimate made for Norway [1] suggests that the maximum margin of error in the national product figures since 1930 is
± 3 per cent; in the figures for 1900–1930, ± 7–8 per cent; and
around 1865, ± 20 per cent.

There are, however, some reasons for confidence in the figures.
From 1901 onwards, movements in national product can be
compared with movements in industrial production. This provides some independent check. Although they may share a number of common sources, the industrial production series are based
mainly on physical quantities with value weights, and the national product series are value figures deflated by a price index;
the two series are therefore to some extent independent. Further
in most of our countries they are, to a considerable extent, different ways of measuring the same thing; for industrial production accounts directly for a substantial part of the national
product, and a good deal of the remainder tends to move in line
with it—items such as freight transport and distribution. The

1. Jul Bjerke, *Some Aspects of Long-term Economic Growth of Norway
since* 1865, paper presented to the 6th European Conference of the International Association for Research in Income and Wealth, August 1959.

industrial production series do in fact tend to confirm the national product series. The direction and the turning points are nearly always the same, but—as might be expected—the industrial series show both steeper cyclical swings and a more rapid secular growth.

GROWTH AND POPULATION

It is the rise in output per man-year, much more than any increase in population, which has accounted for the increase in the national products of these countries over the last 50–100 years (Table 2). In Sweden, for instance, the population increase explains only a quarter of the rise in output, and in France hardly any of it. Canada, the Netherlands and the United States are exceptions; here the population rise was important and explains about half the increase in total production.

Further, there is not much evidence to support the commonly-held belief that a stable population is an important obstacle to growth. Kuznets found, from a comparison of the figures for nineteen countries, that there was no clear-cut association between rates of population growth and product per head of total population.[2] The present study also shows only a tentative and inconclusive association between rate of growth of output per head and that of population of working age; neither over the whole period nor in either sub-period before or after 1913 is there any significant correlation. It is true that the two immigrant countries, the United States and Canada, show both rapid population rises and also high rates of economic growth. But it is Japan, ranking fourth in growth of working population, and Sweden, ranking tenth, which are at the top of the list of productivity increases. The United Kingdom, France and Italy rank low in the rate of growth both of population of working age and of production per man year; but the Netherlands, which had the most rapid population growth of the non-immigrant countries, also had the slowest growth of total product per man-year.

If we look at the changes in the rates for separate countries between the periods before and after 1913, there is a slight and tentative suggestion that a slowing down in economic growth

2. See S. Kuznets, 'Levels and Variability of Rates of Growth', *Economic Development and Cultural Change*, vol. 5, no. 1, October 1956.

TABLE 2. *Rates of Growth of Working-age Population and National Product per Man-Year*

	Starting year	Ranking in total period			Annual per cent increases						
		Product per man-year	Working-age population	Total product	Total period			Up to 1913		1913–1959	
					Product per man-year	Working-age population	Total product	Product per man-year	Working-age population	Product per man-year	Working-age population
Japan	1880	1	4	1	2.9	1.2	4.0	3.4	0.9	2.6	1.4
Sweden	1863	2	10	4	2.1	0.7	2.8	2.4	0.7	1.7	0.8
United States	1871	3	2	2	2.0	1.7	3.8	2.2	2.3	1.8	1.2
Canada	1872	4	1	3	1.7	1.8	3.5	1.9	2.1	1.5	1.6
Denmark	1872	5	6	5	1.6	1.0	2.6	2.1	1.1	1.2	1.0
Norway	1865	6	7	8	1.6	0.9	2.5	1.3	0.8	1.9	1.0
France	1855	7	11	11	1.5	0.1	1.5	1.5	0.1	1.5	0.1
Germany	1853	8	5	7	1.5	1.1	2.5	1.5	1.1	1.4	1.1
Italy	1863	9	8	10	1.2	0.8	1.8	0.7	0.6	1.7	0.9
United Kingdom	1857	10	9	9	1.2	0.7	2.0	1.6	1.0	0.8	0.5
Netherlands	1900	11	3	6	1.1	1.4	2.5	0.7	1.5	1.3	1.4

Note: From 1913 onwards product per man-year is obtained by dividing the national product not by the working-age population but by the employed population. For this reason, both for the period 1913–1959 and for the whole period, the changes in population and in product per man-year do not exactly make up the change in the total product. But the differences are very small.

goes with a slowing down in the rise in population, and vice versa. But it does not follow that it was the change in population growth which influenced economic growth; it could as well have been the other way round, or the association may have been accidental.

Six countries have slower rates of economic growth after 1913 than they did before it; and of these, three—Canada, the United States and Britain—also show a significant decline in the rate of population growth. But for two of them, the United States and Canada, it may well be that the change in the trend of immigration was partly influenced by the fact that their economies were growing more slowly for other reasons.

France had a virtually stationary population and about the same rate of growth in both periods. Of the three remaining countries, Norway and Italy had higher rates of growth after 1913 than before it; so did Japan, up till 1941. In all three, the population also rose faster after 1913. Norway and Italy do not appear to have started sustained economic growth until nearly the end of the 19th century and Japan started from an extremely low level. It is certainly possible that population increases stimulated growth in these countries; it is also possible that improvement of very low living standards stimulated population increase through a reduction of the death rate.

This analysis does not exclude the possibility that a rapid rise in population may stimulate output per man in certain circumstances; but it certainly does not suggest that this has been a major determining factor in the last hundred years. There is absolutely no indication that it is a necessary condition of economic growth; some of the fastest growing countries have had relatively stable populations.

GROWTH THROUGH CATACLYSMS: 1913–1959

Since 1913 normal economic development has been drastically affected by three cataclysms—the two world wars and the great depression. It has been suggested that some kind of normal growth rate runs through such major disturbances; and that there is 'a general principle observed in the figures for all countries, for all recoveries from wars and other major upheavals. Growth is naturally much more rapid than usual until the country gets back on its trend line, after which the normal rate of growth is resumed.'[3] Of this there is little evidence. Our series do suggest that growth is especially fast during the recovery period following a major interruption, but that, at least during the twentieth century, countries have never fully made up the ground they lost as a result of the cataclysms.

Consequently the average growth rates of the period since 1913 are not of much use.

In studying economic growth in order to speculate about the future it is obviously not very reasonable to expect a repetition of the great depression; nor is it sensible to assume that—if there is another world war—its economic effects would be some sort of statistical average of the effects of the last two. It is not helpful to incorporate into the answers to hypothetical questions about the future the same number and kind of cataclysms as occurred in an arbitrarily-chosen period of the past.

For the different experience of the various countries in the two world wars and the great depression thoroughly distorted their growth rates. Canada and the United States show higher rates of growth in the combined war period than they do in peacetime. Norway, Sweden, Denmark, Italy and the Netherlands all show some net growth in the two world wars, but at rates ranging from less than a quarter to about a half of their peace-time average. The other four countries show either very slow growth rates or actual falls in output for the war periods together (Table 3).

The effect of these wartime variations is such that neither the long-term rates of growth including the wars, nor the peacetime rates excluding them, can be regarded in any sense as normal. For if we regard the rates over the whole period as normal, it must be because we believe that in peacetime countries made up for their losses in wartime. If this were so, countries whose output fell sharply during the wars would show particularly rapid peacetime rates of growth. Alternatively, if we believe that the peacetime average gives normal growth rates, this must mean that we believe that the peacetime rates were not affected by wartime experience.

Our results suggest, tentatively, something between these two hypotheses: that the nations particularly hard hit in the war

3. Colin Clark, *Financial Times*, 8 June 1960.

TABLE 3. *Rates of Growth in National Product per Man-Year,*
1913–1959, Peacetime and Wartime Experience

Annual per cent increases

	Total period 1913–1959	Peace-time			War-time average	Ranking		
		1922–1938	1950–1959	Peace-time average		Total period	Peace average	War average
Japan	2.6	4.4	6.1	5.0	−0.1	1	1	9
Norway	1.9	2.6	3.1	2.8	0.9	2	4	3
United States	1.8	1.1	2.2	1.5	2.2	3	10	1
Italy	1.7	1.7	4.7	2.8	0.5	4	3	7
Sweden	1.7	2.7(a)	2.8	2.7	0.6	5	5	6
Canada	1.5	0.6	2.0	1.1	1.9	6	11	2
France	1.5	1.8	3.6	2.4	0.3	7	6	8
Germany	1.4	3.3(b)	4.5	3.8	−0.8	8	2	11
Netherlands	1.3	0.8	3.4	1.7	0.7	9	7	5
Denmark	1.2	1.5	1.8	1.6	0.7	10	8	4
United Kingdom	0.8	1.5	1.7	1.6	−0.2	11	9	10

Note: Both on account of breaks in the figures, and in order to exclude the period of starting up again after the wars, the "wartime" rates have been taken as covering the years 1913 to 1922 and 1938 to 1950. For Sweden the first world war period is taken as 1913 to 1923, and for Germany 1913 to 1925. Owing to the major difficulty of establishing price links between pre-war and post-war periods for countries with major currency upsets, there is a considerably wider margin of error in the wartime average than in the peacetime periods and the rates shown should only be taken as giving the general direction and magnitude of the change. The margin of error in the wartime changes may in some countries be sufficient to affect the 1913–59 average significantly, although its weight in this average is probably not sufficient to change the order of magnitude seriously.
(a) 1923–38.   (b) 1925–38.

may have caught up to some extent in peacetime, but not completely. Canada and the United States, the two countries that grew faster in wartime than peacetime, had the slowest peacetime rates of growth. All the nine countries which had a marked loss of growth in wartime grew faster in peacetime than the United States and Canada. But the catching-up was by no means complete: among the nine countries themselves, there is little evidence that those particularly hard hit by the war did particularly well in peacetime.

The analysis of the effects of the great depression suggests similar results (Table 4)—that there was some catching up afterwards, but that it was not complete: consequently the period spanning the depression, from about 1929 to 1937,[4] cannot be regarded as normal either. First, by 1937 or 1938 most countries had by no means regained the trend indicated by their growth rates up to 1929; 1929–1937 rates were relatively low for most countries, and very low indeed for some. The ground lost in the great depression was in general not made up. Further, there is some tendency, though not a strong one, for the countries worst hit by the depression to show relatively low growth rates over the whole inter-war period. The two countries whose output dropped most in the depression—Canada and the United States —rank seventh and ninth respectively in their inter-war growth rates.

But, although recovery from the depression was clearly not complete, there were some very strong recovery effects: it was, on the whole, the countries whose output had fallen most sharply in the recession which showed the most rapid rates of rise after 1932. So there is no question of using the period 1932–1937 as in any way a normal period: it was dominated by the after-effects of the depression.

THE PERIOD BEFORE 1913

Since the period after 1913 is so disturbed, if we are to find

4. As growth was again interrupted in a number of countries by the recession in 1938, the post-depression period has been taken only up to 1937 for all countries except Japan. Two alternative definitions of national income for Japan produce different movements between 1937 and 1938. The movement over the whole period from 1933 until 1938 appears, however, to be moderately well established.

TABLE 4. Growth Rates and the Depression: 1922-1938

Annual per cent increases

| | Total period 1922(a)-1938 | | Before and after 1929(b) | | | | Depression and recovery | | | Period of depression |
| | | | 1922(a)-1929(b) | | 1929(b)-1937(c) | | Depression: total product, trough as per cent of previous peak | Trough of depression to 1937(c) | | |
	Total product	Product per man-year	Total product	Product per man-year	Total product	Product per man-year		Total product	Product per man-year	
Japan	5.2	4.4	6.5	5.9	3.6	2.4	no fall	4.8	3.7	1931–1933
Germany	4.0	3.3	5.7	6.0	2.8	2.1	84	8.8	3.5	1928–1932
Sweden	3.1	2.7	3.9	3.3	2.3	1.9	87	6.3	4.6	1930–1932
Norway	3.2	2.6	3.9	3.1	2.5	2.0	92	4.3	3.4	1930–1931
France	1.4	1.8	5.8	5.8	−2.1	−1.3	82	(d)	(d)	1929–1936
Italy	1.9	1.7	2.3	2.2	1.9	1.6	95	3.0	2.7	1929–1930
Denmark	2.8	1.5	3.6	2.1	2.0	1.1	98	2.8	0.4	1931–1932
United Kingdom	2.3	1.5	2.7	1.6	2.3	1.6	94	4.9	2.2	1929–1932
United States	1.8	1.1	4.8	2.1	0.1	0.4	70	9.7	4.9	1929–1933
Netherlands	1.8	0.8	4.0	2.0	0.2	0.3	88	5.0	3.4	1929–1934
Canada	2.1	0.6	5.1	2.1	−0.3	−0.9	71	8.4	3.9	1929–1933

(a) From 1925 for Germany and from 1923 for Sweden.
(b) Or year of onset of depression if other than 1929.
(c) 1938 for Japan.
(d) No recovery until 1936.

any historical experience which might be relevant for future growth rates we must look at the period before the first world war. Here the problems of comparison are most acute. Not only is the margin of error in the figures much higher, but we are looking at a different kind of world, with many of our countries still in an early stage of industrialisation. Do the rates of economic growth found in these circumstances have any relevance to present conditions? And if so, are they appropriately measured by today's national accounting conventions?

Fortunately we do not need to try to compare the level of production of 1870 with that in 1960, when we would have the problem of comparing worlds with radically different products: hansom cabs and oil-lamps as against taxis and electricity. Rather we are comparing the rate of growth between, say, 1870 and 1880 with that between 1950 and 1960, and the problems of the introduction of new commodities and techniques are much smaller. In every period growth is affected by the rate of innovation, and it is true that the earlier period was for many countries one of particularly rapid technological change; but this has also been true of the nineteen-fifties.

In one respect, however, nineteenth century economic growth does differ substantially from that of later periods. Part of total economic growth is explained by changes in the distribution of the labour force, in particular the shift from low-paid occupations such as agriculture and domestic service to higher-paid occupations in industry. This shift was very important in the nineteenth century and for some countries in the first quarter of the twentieth century; by the end of the second world war it had almost come to an end in most of our countries, except Japan. For most of the countries we do not have enough information to separate out that part of the total productivity increase which can be attributed to labour force shifts. There are, however, some figures for the United States: it has been estimated that, since 1910, about one-eighth to one-quarter of the total long-term increase in productivity was due to such shifts.

Growth rates calculated from these early series may be too high because the share of sectors which are declining, or growing more slowly than the rest, is underestimated. This is likely because there is much more information about the industrial,

rapidly-expanding sectors than about the agricultural and handi-
craft sectors. The use of modern national accounting conventions
can also lead to overestimates of growth in these earlier periods.
National accounting figures in general include only market transactions. In less developed countries more needs are satisfied
within the family. Consequently there is a difficulty when we
calculate changes over time in output per head of population of
working age. Throughout, family workers are included in the
population, but their non-market product may be excluded from
national output. Over a period, therefore, when the share of the
non-market product in the total was falling, the increase in output per head is overestimated.

These are the qualifications to bear in mind in considering the
figures in Tables 5 and 6. The averages for the whole period before 1913 must be treated cautiously, because they cover very
different periods for different countries—periods ranging from
thirty to sixty years. But it is not sensible—as it is for 1913–1959
—to compare common chronological sub-periods for these countries; for whereas from 1913 onwards two world wars and a great
depression dominated the economic trend in all the countries
considered here, before 1913 each country's economic development was largely determined by its domestic circumstances. For
instance, the United Kingdom and Sweden, which had been the
fastest growing countries in the late 'sixties and early 'seventies,
were stagnating in the late 'seventies; this was the time when Germany and the United States were growing very fast indeed—
Germany after the achievement of political unity and the United
States after the American Civil War.

Nor is it possible to isolate with any certainty periods in the
history of each country at which they could be said to be in the
same stage of economic development. By the middle of the nineteenth century the United Kingdom and France had left their
pre-industrial patterns of economic activity far behind. Our
series for Germany and Italy are long enough to show a clear
change of trend: Germany immediately after attaining political
unity and Italy a good deal later. (For these two countries it is
probably useful to exclude the earlier, more slowly growing
period.) For the other countries there is tentative evidence that
some of our series start around the first period of intensive in-

TABLE 5. *Rapid Growth Rates of National Product per Man-Year Before 1913* (a)

Annual per cent increases

	Long-term average growth rate, to 1913		Fastest 8-year periods of growth		Periods (b) during which growth exceeded			
					2½ per cent a year		3 per cent a year	
	Starting-year	Rate	Period	Rate	Period	No. years	Period	No. years
Japan	1880	3.4	1891–99	4.7	1880–1911	31	1880–1911	31
Sweden	1863	2.4	1880–88 1866–74 1890–98 1900–08	4.5 4.6 2.9 2.8	1866–98 1900–11	32 11	1863–75 1891–98 1903–08	12 7 5
United States	1871	2.2	1872–80	5.2	1871–1907	36	1871–89	18
Denmark	1872	2.1	1896–1904 1877–85 1888–96	3.1 2.4 2.4	1877–84 1887–93 1895–99	7 6 4	1896–1905 1878–82 1887–90	9 4 3
Canada	1872	1.9	1875–83 1895–1903	4.1 2.2	1874–90 1899–1904	16 5	1874–86	12
United Kingdom	1857	1.6	1867–75 1881–89	2.7 2.5	1859–73 1881–89	14 8	1867–73	6
Germany	1853	1.5	1874–82 1882–90	3.5 2.0	1873–93	20	1873–86	13
Norway (a)	1865	1.3	1905–13	2.7	1905–13	8	1909–13	4
Italy	1863	0.7	1871–77 1897–1905	2.4 (c) 2.3	1898–1902 1904–07	4 3	—	—

(a) The long-term rate is calculated up to the year 1913. All other dates refer to the centre of five year averages; for instance, 1911 = 1909–13. For Norway however, the rates are calculated from single years. (b) Of three years or more. (c) As the series only covers selected years, only a six year period is available.

TABLE 6. *Comparisons of Growth Rates of National Product per Man-Year*

	1950–1959	1954–1959	1922[a]–1929[b]	Fastest 8 years before 1913	Pre-1913 average	Post-1913 average
	A. Annual per cent increases					
Japan	6.1	7.6	5.9	4.7	3.4	2.6
Italy	4.7	3.8	2.2	2.3	0.7	1.7
Germany	4.5	3.6	6.0	3.5	1.5	1.4
France	3.6	3.3	5.8	..	1.5	1.5
Netherlands	3.4	2.9	2.0	(c)	(c)	1.3
Norway	3.1	2.5	3.1	2.7	1.3	1.9
Sweden	2.8	3.0	3.3	4.6	2.4	1.7
United States	2.2	2.2	2.1	5.2	2.2	1.8
Canada	2.0	1.8	2.1	4.1	1.9	1.5
Denmark	1.8	2.5	2.1	2.4	2.1	1.2
United Kingdom	1.7	1.6	1.6	2.7	1.6	0.8
	B. Ranking					
Japan	1	1	2	2	1	1
Italy	2	2	6	9	10	4
Germany	3	3	1	5	7	8
France	4	4	3	..	8	7
Netherlands	5	6	10	(c)	(c)	(c)
Norway	6	7	5	6	9	2
Sweden	7	5	4	3	2	5
United States	8	9	7	1	3	3
Canada	9	10	8	4	5	6
Denmark	10	8	9	8	4	9
United Kingdom	11	11	11	7	6	10

(a) From 1925 for Germany, and from 1923 for Sweden.
(b) Or the onset of the depression (Table 4).
(c) Omitted because pre-1913 figures only cover thirteen years.

dustrialisation.[5] Some of these countries, however, seem to have entered the phase of industrialisation with a short period of very rapid growth, and others much more gradually.

The periods which it does seem useful to isolate, from pre-1913 experience, are the fastest growing periods in each country— since a number of our questions are concerned with rapid rates of growth. Table 5 sets out for each country the two or three

5. For a number of countries our series start very near the time identified by Rostow as 'take-off'. See W. W. Rostow, *Stages of Economic Growth*, Cambridge University Press, 1960.

eight-year periods of most rapid growth before 1913; it also shows for how long at a stretch the various countries did in fact exceed growth rates of 2½ and 3 per cent.

CONCLUSIONS

The amount we can learn from past growth rates that is relevant to prediction about the future is limited. Our tools of measurement are crude, both because of conceptual limitations and because our figures on actual movements are still, in spite of recent improvement, subject to a wide margin of error. Most of the lessons of this study are negative—in that they suggest that some of the simple relationships that have been put forward do not hold good.

There is little evidence of a direct connection between the increase in output per man and the increase in population; and where there is an association it may be that it is the rise in the standard of living which explains the rise in population rather than the other way round. In any case, a rise in population is clearly not an essential condition of economic growth; some of the fastest growing countries have had relatively slow population growth.

There is no convincing evidence of any constancy or normality in the international pattern of growth rates (Table 6); almost any hypothesis of constancy which one tries on the figures gets a negative answer—with the one exception that Japan, in almost any period one selects, comes at the top of the table. Apart from Japan, there is no connection between the ranking of countries before and after 1913; this remains true whether or not the German and Italian figures are adjusted by excluding their early periods of slow growth. Nor is there any correlation between those countries which had the fastest spurts in the nineteenth century and those which have grown fastest since the second world war. There is some constancy in ranking if we compare 1922–1929 with either 1950–1959 or 1954–1959. The sensible explanation of this may be that in both periods the same group of countries were making rather delayed recoveries from the severe damage caused by war.

It is not safe to say—on the basis of a single comparison of pre-1913 and post-1913 averages—that growth rates are slowing down secularly. For although it is true that the post-1913 averages are lower, this can perfectly well be explained by the three cataclysms in the twentieth century. It is true that since 1950 it is the richest nations which have shown the slowest growth (Table 1): this might suggest that, after a certain point, the transfer of working population from the manufacturing sector to the service sector could have a slowing down effect. But it is far too soon, on the basis of nine years' figures, to be certain about this.

Nor can we classify countries into one group which normally grows fast and one group which normally grows slowly. Nearly all countries—again, except Japan—have had fairly long periods of both rapid growth and slow growth. At one time or another, every country except two has grown for eight years or more at a rate faster than 3 per cent a year; one of the exceptions—Britain —reached 2.7 per cent for the eight years before 1875, and 3 per cent for six of them.

These apparently negative conclusions are, in a way, encouraging: there is no suggestion of any long-term historical inevitability about growth rates. Countries which for a long time had ranked low in the list have succeeded in changing their ranking. For instance, if this article had been written ten years ago, it might have been tempting to conclude that Italy could not grow fast: before the second world war, she had never reached 2½ per cent a year for more than four years at a time.[6] Since 1950 she has ranked second, with an average growth rate of over 4½ per cent for nine years. The countries which have ranked low since 1950 have all had long periods in which they grew faster. Britain, for instance, enjoyed a continuous period of about forty-five years from 1857 in which her average growth rate was above that of 1950–1959; and the United States exceeded her post-war growth rate for forty years together.

Japan appears to be the one exception to the rule that there are no obvious rules; she is the country that has consistently grown faster than the others through nearly all the period. This may be due to a substantial extent to the fact that, in an economy starting from a very low level, the necessity of competing in foreign markets led to a higher degree of concentration of investment and the development of a small but relatively productive modern manu-

6. Except for the few years of recovery from the great depression.

facturing sector, which, owing to the particular social and institutional pattern, has continued to develop side by side with
very much less productive domestic manufacture and agriculture.[7] Consequently productivity gains have been made on a
much larger scale than in other countries by the transfer of
workers to more productive sectors, as well as by rising productivity in each sector.[8] This process of transfer is still incom-
plete, and consequently rapid increases in productivity are still
to be expected.[9] The Japanese long-run plan is for a growth rate
in real national product per head of population of 6.9 per cent a
year from 1956–58 to 1970.[10] They expect that the proportion of
the labour force engaged in agriculture and other primary industry will fall from 40 to 23 per cent.

Do the historical figures throw any light on the 1950–1959
rapid rates of growth? First of all, these rapid rates are not unprecedented (Table 6). France was growing faster and Japan
almost as fast in the period from 1922 to the depression. It is
true that Italy had not herself previously grown as fast as 4.7
per cent a year for eight years, nor had Germany reached 4.5
per cent except in the very short period from 1925 to 1928. These
two countries had no precedent in their own histories. But other
countries had reached figures as high as these before—the United
States and Sweden, for example. Nothing very exceptional has
happened yet.

But hitherto it is true that growth rates of over 3 per cent a
year for more than eight years have always been in periods when
there was some special explanation—such as political integration
or recovery from a war. This, together with the similarity between 1922–1929 and 1950–1959, does suggest that there may
well be exceptional recovery factors in these recent rapid rates.
It is noticeable that for all the fastest growing countries except

7. Kiyoshi Kojima, 'Capital Accumulation and the Course of Industrialisation, with Special Reference to Japan', *Economic Journal*, December 1960.

8. The upward bias to the figures which derives from the exclusion of
the non-market product and from the underestimate of some slowly-
growing sectors probably affects the Japanese figures more than those of
the other countries.

9. Since, however, we expect these high rates to be due largely to an
extension of the most productive sector, it does not follow that Japanese
productivity within the modern factory sector will increase more rapidly
than that of other countries.

10. *New Long-range Economic Plan for Japan*, Economic Planning
Agency, published by Japan Times, Tokyo, 1961.

Japan the 1954–1959 rates are lower than the 1950–1959 averages.

Though nothing exceptional or unprecedented has happened yet, it will be unprecedented if the rapid post-war rates are continued for another ten or fifteen years. It would be unwise to assume, on the basis of historical experience, that this is in any way impossible. There are a large number of forces now making for higher rates of growth which did not exist before: the absence of prolonged depressions, the competition between capitalist and communist economic systems, and the development of incentives to fast growth, including techniques of planning which can be applied to predominantly free enterprise economies. Within Western Europe the economic integration now in process may be as stimulating to growth as it was when, for instance, Germany was united.

It is naive to regard a process as complex as the expansion of economic output as following some necessarily predetermined pattern; the main lesson of the historical figures is simply that no such pattern does in fact appear in them. When a farmer is estimating probable crop yields he will be wise to assume that these will be subject to the same climatic and other variations as in the past, but foolish to assume that statistical averages of past yields represent the most probable yield under improved conditions of fertilisation and irrigation.

PART THREE   How to Grow: Three Kinds of Investment

Growth Through Taxation

JAMES TOBIN

James Tobin contributed this essay in 1960 to The New Republic *shortly before becoming a member of the Council of Economic Advisers under President Kennedy. He has since returned to Yale University, where he is Sterling Professor of Economics.*

THE OVERRIDING issue of political economy in the 1960's is how to allocate the national output. How much to private consumption? How much for private investment in plant and equipment? For government investment and public services? For national defense? For foreign aid and overseas investment? Though our productive capacity is great and is growing, the demands upon it seem to be growing even faster.

The allocation of resources among competing uses is *the* central and classical theoretical problem of economics. Likewise it is the inescapable central practical problem of a Soviet-type planned economy, or of any economy under the forced draft of total war. Only recently has allocation of the output of the peacetime American economy begun to emerge from economics texts into the political arena, as a challenge and opportunity for democratic decision and governmental action. Public economic policy and debate have long been dominated by other concerns: unemployment, inflation, inequality. The composition of national output has been an unintended byproduct rather than a conscious objective of economic policy.

The importance of accelerating economic growth brings the question of allocation to the fore. Can we as a nation, by political decision and governmental action, increase our rate of growth? Or must the rate of growth be regarded fatalistically, the result of uncoordinated decisions and habits of millions of consumers, businessmen, and governments, uncontrollable in our kind of society except by exhortation and prayer? The communists are telling the world that they alone know how to mobilize economic resources for rapid growth. The appeal of free institutions in the underdeveloped world, and perhaps even their survival in the West, may depend on whether the communists are right. We cannot, we need not leave the outcome to chance.

USING OUR CAPACITY FOR GROWTH

How can an increase in the rate of growth of national output be achieved? The answer is straightforward and painful. We must devote more of our current capacity to uses that increase our future capacity, and correspondingly less to other uses. The uses of current capacity that build up future productive capacity are of three major types: (1) *Investment:* replacement and expansion of the country's stock of productive capital—factories, machines, roads, trucks, school buildings, hospitals, power dams, pipelines, etc. (2) *Research,* both in basic science and in industrial application, by government, private industry, and non-profit institutions, leading sooner or later to more efficient processes and new products. (3) *Education* of all kinds augmenting the skill of the future labor force. The competing uses of current capacity are: (1) *Unemployment:* failure to employ current capacity to the full, letting potential production be lost through unemployment. (2) *Consumption,* where most of our resources are engaged, providing us with the goods, services, and leisure that constitute the most luxurious standard of living the world has known.

Since 1953 the economy has been operating at an average unemployment level of over 5% of the labor force. A society geared to the objective of growth should keep the average unemployment rate down to 3%. Reduction of unemployment to this level could increase Gross National Product from the current labor force and capital stock by about 20 billion dollars. But this increase in output will contribute to economic growth only if it is used in substantial part for investment, research, and education; it will make no contribution if it is all consumed.

To stimulate growth we must somehow engineer two shifts in the composition of actual and potential national output. One is from private consumption to the public sector, federal, state, and local. Domestic economic growth is, of course, not the only reason for such a shift. Increased defense, increased foreign aid, increased public consumption are possibly equally urgent reasons.

The second shift of resources that must be engineered is from private consumption to private investment. About three quarters of Gross National Product is produced with the help of business plant and equipment. Faster growth of output requires a more rapidly expanding and more up-to-date stock of plant and equipment. Every $1.00 increase of GNP requires in the neighborhood of $1.50 new plant and equipment investment. Thus to raise the rate of growth two percentage points, say from 3% to 5% per annum, the share of plant and equipment investment in current GNP must rise by three percentage points, e.g., from 10% to 13%.

Between 1953 and 1959 potential GNP rose from 365 to an estimated 500 billion dollars. Some of the potential increase went to waste in unemployment. Of the realized increase, 69% went into consumption, 13% into government activity, and 18% into investment.

Unfortunately these calculations *understate* the effective growth of consumption relative to government and investment. The reason is that the prices of goods and services needed for government activity and private investment rose relative to the prices of consumption goods and services. For example, the services of government employees (teachers, policemen, clerks, etc.) rose in price 34% while consumer prices rose 9%. Although we managed to increase government expenditure for such services by 13 billion dollars, 11 billion dollars of the increase was simply the higher cost of the volume of services we were already getting in 1953 and only 2 billion represented a real expansion of such services. When account is taken of this and other unfavorable relative price changes, some 92% of the growth in output "in constant dollars" went to consumption; *government activity actually diminished;* private investment got 16% of the increase in GNP, and *none of this increase was for plant and equipment.*

This suggests we will probably have to continue to do some running just to stay in the same place. Even if we resolve to increase to 25% the government share of that output, and to

18% the investment share, the likely price increases in those sectors would nullify part of those increases.

POLICY MEASURES FOR GROWTH

Policy to accelerate growth must be double-edged. On the one hand, it must stimulate the desired government and private expenditures. On the other hand, it must discourage consumption. Here are some major constituents of a program for growth:

1. Increased expenditure by federal, state, and local governments for education, basic and applied research, urban redevelopment, resource conservation and development, transportation and other public facilities.

2. Stimulus to private investment expenditures by:

(a) Federal Reserve and Treasury policy to create and maintain "easy money" conditions, with credit readily available and interest rates low, especially in long-term capital markets.

(b) Improvement of averaging and loss-offset provisions in taxation of corporate income, in order to increase the degree to which the tax collector shares the risk of investment as well as the reward.

(c) The privilege of deducting from corporate net income for tax purposes a certain percentage of a corporation's outlays for plant and equipment to the extent that these outlays exceed a specified minimum. The specified minimum would be the sum of depreciation and (on the assumption that the tax rate is 52%) 48% of net income before tax. To qualify for the tax concession, a corporation would have to be investing more than its normal gross profits after tax. The concession, and the minimum requirement for eligibility for it, are designed to encourage greater corporate saving, the full investment of internal funds, and, most important, the undertaking of investment financed by outside saving obtained from the capital market. An analogous proposal to encourage non-corporate saving and investment is suggested below.

If these measures were adopted, a reduction in the basic corporate income tax rate, advocated by many as essential to growth, would be neither necessary nor equitable. Indeed the strength of these measures might be greater if the rate were increased.

3. Restriction of consumption, by:

(a) Increase in personal income tax at all levels, accompanied by permission to deduct a certain amount of saving from income subject to tax. Like present deductions for charity, medical care, etc., the saving deduction would be claimed at the taxpayer's option, with the burden of proof on him. A schedule of "normal" saving for taxpayers of various incomes and family circumstances would be established, and only saving in excess of a taxpayer's "normal" would be eligible for deduction. A scheme of this kind seems to be the most feasible equitable way to use the tax instrument to favor saving at the expense of consumption.

(b) Improvements in the social security system—e.g., raising retirement benefits and relating their amount, above a common minimum, to cumulated covered earnings—should be introduced on a quasi-contributory basis. Since the payroll tax contributions then precede the benefits, the funds accumulate and can be an important channel of national saving.

(c) Increases in state and local taxes—property or sales or income as the case may be—to keep pace with the share of these governments in the necessary expansion of the public sector.

(d) Limitation, to a reasonable proportion of sales, of the privilege of deducting advertising and promotional expenses from corporate income subject to tax. No observer of the American scene doubts that advertising is excessive. From the economic point of view, it absorbs too large a share of the nation's resources itself, and at the same time it generates synthetic pressures for ever-higher consumption.

RESTRAINING THE INCREASE OF CONSUMPTION

Increased taxation is the price of growth. We must tax ourselves not only to finance the necessary increase in public expenditures but also to finance, indirectly, the expansion of private investment. A federal budget surplus is a method by which we as a nation can expand the volume of saving available for private investment beyond the current saving of individuals and corporations. The surplus must, to be sure, be coupled with measures to stimulate investment, so that the national resolution to save actually leads to capital formation and is not wasted in unemployment and unrequited loss of consumption. It is only superficially paradoxical to combine anti-inflationary fiscal policy with an expansionary monetary policy. The policies outlined above must be combined in the right proportions, so that aggregate demand is high enough to maintain a 3% unemployment rate but not higher. There are several mixtures which can do that job; of them we must choose the one that gives the desired composition of aggregate demand. If the overwhelming problem of democratic capitalism in the '30's and even the '50's was to bring the business cycle under social control, the challenge of the '60's is to bring under public decision the broad allocation of national output. Fortunately the means are at hand. They are techniques well within the peacetime scope of government. We can do the job without the direct controls of wartime—priorities, rationing, price and wage controls.

The means are at hand; to use them we will need to muster more wisdom, maturity, leadership, and sense of national purpose than we displayed in the '50's. A program which allows an increase of per capita consumption of about 1% a year would scarcely be a program of austerity. Indeed it would not even feel austere if the growth of gross output per head were held to 1½% per annum. We are used to institutions that let us realize in increased consumption about two-thirds of increases in output. But let people earn the incomes associated with a 2½% rise in output per capita, and the measures necessary to keep their consumption from rising faster than 1% may seem burdensome sacrifices. Our communist competitors have an advantage. Since they do not pay out such increases in output as personal incomes in the first place, they do not have the problem of recapturing them in taxes or saving. That problem we cannot escape in a free society. Unless we master it, we shall not fare well in the competition for economic growth and national survival.

Tangible Investment as an Instrument of Growth

EDMUND S. PHELPS

This essay, which was written expressly for this volume, is based on "The New View of Investment" which appeared in the November 1962 issue of The Quarterly Journal of Economics *and other contributions of the author on the relation between investment and growth.*

How EFFECTIVE is tangible investment as an instrument for economic growth? This paper surveys some recent developments in the way economists have conceived of capital and examines the implications of these ideas for productivity and growth.

THE WORLD OF HARROD AND DOMAR

One of the most important "models" of the relation of investment to growth is due to Roy F. Harrod of Oxford and Evsey D. Domar of the Massachusetts Institute of Technology. They postulated that capital and output must grow in the same proportion. Let the ratio of capital, K, to annual capacity output, Q, be denoted by the constant β. Then

$$K = \beta Q \tag{1}$$

Therefore, if we want to raise our productive capacity by one dollar we shall need β dollars' worth of additional capital. In general, an increase ΔQ in annual capacity requires a capital-stock increase ΔK equal to $\beta \cdot \Delta Q$:

$$\Delta K = \beta \cdot \Delta Q \tag{2}$$

Let us measure the increases ΔK and ΔQ from the start of the calendar year. Then ΔK is just the annual amount of investment net of replacement—or the "annual rate of net investment." We say *net* investment, for if some existing capital has to be retired during the year it will be necessary to invest (so-called replacement investment) just to keep the capital stock from decreasing. Clearly the rate at which output capacity grows each year depends upon the annual rate of net investment. Suppose that each year the community saves and invests, net of replacement, a constant proportion, s, of its output (income). That is,

$$\Delta K = sQ, \qquad 0 \leqq s \leqq 1 \tag{3}$$

From these relationships we can derive the relative annual rate of growth of capacity output in the economy. Equations (2) and (3) tell us that $\beta \cdot \Delta Q = sQ$. Hence, dividing both sides of this equality by Q and β, we obtain the simple growth-rate formula:

$$\frac{\Delta Q}{Q} = \frac{s}{\beta} \tag{4}$$

This seemingly optimistic formula states that we can have (in perpetuity) any desired growth rate merely by choosing the appropriate fraction of our income (output) to save and invest. Suppose that $s = 9\%$ and that $\beta = 3.0$. Then the growth rate would be 3% per annum. If we wished to grow twice as fast, just multiply the target growth rate of 6% by β to obtain 18% as the required s. It suffices to double the rate of net investment.

How plausible is this? The answer depends upon the key assumption of a constant capital-output ratio. Is this assumption reasonable? Does it need to be qualified?

It is clear that if we were to interpret the ratio of output to capital as an immutable constant—one independent of the size of the labor force—this would mean that labor made no contribution to output. It would mean that capital was the only scarce factor of production. But we know that labor is scarce because it commands a positive price (wage) in the marketplace. No employer would pay for an input which was not productive. So the single-factor interpretation of the constancy of the capital-output ratio is untenable.

The Fixed Factor Proportions Assumption · The standard version of the Harrod-Domar model treats both labor and capital as necessary factors of production. How then can the capital-output ratio still be treated as constant?

Exponents of this standard version of the model suppose that capital and labor are perfectly *complementary*: every "machine" needs a fixed complement of men operating it if it is to produce, and there is only one known type of machine. A shovel is an example; a lathe is another. Second, it is supposed that there are constant returns to scale: double employment and capital (the number of machines) and you will double capacity output.

There are clearly only so many machines that this economy can use at any point in time. As long as there are too few machines to go around, additional machines would be useful and output will grow in proportion to capital. But if there is no surplus labor to be combined with more machines, an increase in capital would not increase output: it would only lead to idle machines. *Thus the capital-output ratio is a constant only as long as there is surplus labor.*

Suppose there is surplus labor to begin with and suppose that capital is growing at 6% per annum due to a high-investment policy. Then employment and output will also grow at the rate of 6%. But suppose finally that the available supply of labor is growing at only 1% per annum. Then the economy must eventually run out of surplus labor. The growth path of output will encounter a *ceiling*—in our example, an upward-slanting ceiling. Thereafter, output can grow no faster than the labor supply, no faster than 1%. The investment rate will be reduced since there is no point to producing machines that would have to stand idle. The economy can do no better than crawl along the ceiling output path.

To give plausibility to our numerical example we have to take technical progress into account. Suppose that the output which 100 men can produce today can be performed by only 98 workers tomorrow (with the same amount of capital). Then 2 workers could be released tomorrow to tend new machines. This is as good as having 102 workers tomorrow. The increase in the efficiency of the labor force raises the amount of capital the economy can use in the same manner as an increase in the size of the labor force. We have to add the 2% increase in the efficiency of labor to the 1% increase in the supply of labor to obtain the (3%) growth rate along the ceiling output path. Harrod called this growth-rate concept the *natural* rate of growth to emphasize that it is determined, independently of investment decisions, by deep-seated technologic and demographic trends.

In the Harrod-Domar model, therefore, population and technology impose a ceiling on the capacity output which is achievable at every point in time through tangible investment. Once the labor force becomes fully equipped with machines, output cannot grow faster than the natural rate—the growth rate of the output ceiling—no matter how rapidly we might add to the stock of machines. So the Harrod-Domar model does not make investment so all-powerful after all.

THE NEOCLASSICAL RESURGENCE

The ideas of Harrod and Domar run counter to traditional economic theorizing. Neoclassical theorists like Marshall, Wicksteed and Wicksell would not have accepted the notion that capital and labor were strict complements in the productive process. And modern theorists found it difficult to swallow too. So Robert Solow of M.I.T., Trevor Swan of the Australian National University and James Tobin of Yale led a neoclassical revolt against the Harrod-Domar model.

Neoclassical theory supposes that capital and labor can be *substituted* for each other. Rather than "twenty machines, therefore twenty (or eight or fifty) jobs, and no more," neoclassical theory treats capital as an abstract substance which can be shaped to absorb any size labor force. Whereas Harrod and Domar think of capital as "machines" with rigid labor requirements, the neoclassicals think of capital as putty with which "any number can play."

Given the labor force, the larger is the amount of capital, the larger will be the level of annual output. Each worker will have more putty to work with, so he can produce more. But we have to expect diminishing returns: successive equal increments of capital will (eventually) yield successively smaller increments of output. This contrasts with the Harrod-Domar implication that at first output grows by equal increments and then, once the surplus labor is absorbed, output cannot be further increased. Where the world of Harrod-Domar is kinky and abrupt, the neoclassical domain is smooth and continuous.

This process of increasing the amount of capital per worker, in order to increase output per worker, the neoclassicals called *capital deepening*. The basic neoclassical model of the relation between capital deepening and growth can be presented quite simply.

The neoclassicals start with the notion of a *production function*,

$$Q = f(K, L), \tag{5}$$

which tells us how much output can be produced by a given combination of capital, K, and labor, L.

Second, the neoclassicals usually suppose constant returns to scale. This means, once again, that a 1% increase in both capital and labor will yield a 1% increase in capacity output.

Third, the neoclassicals suppose that pure competition prevails in every corner of the economy.

From these three assumptions it follows that the growth rate of capacity output is a kind of *average* of the growth rates of capital and labor. A "simple" average would add half the growth rate of capital and half the growth rate of labor. But generally the input growth rates must be assigned unequal weights in the averaging process: like one-third of the growth rate of capital plus two-thirds of the growth rate of labor. In symbols the result can be expressed:

$$\frac{\Delta Q}{Q} = a \cdot \frac{\Delta K}{K} + (1-a)\ \frac{\Delta L}{L} \tag{6}$$

What makes the result informative is that the weight attached to each input's growth rate equals the *relative share* of total income (output) received by that input. Thus a is capital's relative share and $1-a$ is the share received in wages.[1]

1. These propositions can be derived quite easily. Any year-to-year increase in the capacity of the economy, ΔQ, must be attributable to the increase, ΔK, in its capital stock and the increase, ΔL, in its labor force. Additions to output are related to increments of input in the following way:

$$\Delta Q = \Delta K \cdot MP_K + \Delta L \cdot MP_L \tag{i}$$

where MP_K and MP_L are the marginal productivities of capital and labor, respectively.

What is marginal productivity? Hold L constant and increase K by one unit; then $\Delta K = 1$ and the increase in output will be $\Delta Q = MP_K$. This is exactly what "marginal productivity" means: the increase in output resulting from a one-unit increase of the input, other inputs remaining unchanged.

Next, let us divide both sides of the equation by Q. Then

$$\frac{\Delta Q}{Q} = \Delta K \frac{MP_K}{Q} + \Delta L \frac{MP_L}{Q} \tag{ii}$$

or, without really changing anything,

$$\frac{\Delta Q}{Q} = \frac{\Delta K}{K}\left(\frac{K \cdot MP_K}{Q}\right) + \frac{\Delta L}{L}\left(\frac{L \cdot MP_L}{Q}\right) \tag{iii}$$

Suppose there are constant returns to scale and pure competition. Under the marginal productivity theory of factor pricing, each unit of input will then be paid its marginal product. Then $K \cdot MP_K$ is just the earnings of capital and $L \cdot MP_L$ the earnings of labor. Together they absorb all the out-

Investment Pessimism · It is easy to see that this neoclassical formula for the rate of growth paints a very different picture from the Harrod-Domar formula. For comparison, we recall that $\Delta K = sQ$ and write the neoclassical formula as follows:

$$\frac{\Delta Q}{Q} = a\frac{s}{K/Q} + (1-a)\frac{\Delta L}{L} \tag{7}$$

Note that capital and labor generate growth independently of one another. For that reason K/Q is no longer treated as a constant (like β). And the term $\frac{s}{K/Q}$ —which we recall appeared in the guise of $\frac{s}{\beta}$ in the Harrod-Domar growth formula, equation (4)—is multiplied by the weight a.[2]

This last point is important. If a should be very small, what good is a large s, what good is investment?

Suppose, as before, that we are growing at 3%, that $K/Q = 3$ and $s = 9\%$. If we double s to 18%, what will happen to the growth rate? If $a = 1$, the growth rate will also double, reaching 6%. But a is approximately equal (we assume) to capital's share of income. This is about one-third. Thus a *doubling* of our rate of net investment, in this example, would raise the growth rate by only one percentage point, to 4%.[3]

Pretty gloomy? Yes, but less so in a sense than Harrod and Domar, who say that there is a ceiling growth path—one that may grow very slowly. At least the neoclassical world offers us the possibility of growing at almost any reasonable rate we might choose if we are sufficiently willing to tighten our belts.

The Importance of Technical Progress · Our concern with growth is not only with the increase of total output but also with the growth of output per worker or labor productivity, $\frac{Q}{L}$.

---

put. Therefore, the weights in (iii), which are the relative shares, add up to one.

2. In this more general neoclassical world, capital growth and labor growth share the credit for growth. But the neoclassical formulation incorporates Harrod and Domar as a special case: If $a = 1$, then output and capital grow in the same proportion and labor is in surplus.

3. Matters are even worse. If $s = 18\%$ and $\frac{K}{Q} = 3.0$, capital will be growing at 6% while output only at 4%. This implies a gradual rise in the K/Q ratio which will slow down the growth rates of capital, hence output.

The relative growth rate of productivity, $\dfrac{\Delta \left(\dfrac{Q}{L}\right)}{\dfrac{Q}{L}}$, is $\dfrac{\Delta Q}{Q} - \dfrac{\Delta L}{L}$.[4]

From our growth-rate equation (6) we derive:

$$\frac{\Delta Q}{Q} - \frac{\Delta L}{L} = a \left(\frac{\Delta K}{K} - \frac{\Delta L}{L}\right) \qquad (8)$$

This equation states that the growth of output per worker requires the growth of capital per worker; that capital's growth rate exceed labor's growth rate. Similarly, we obtain from (6) the growth rate of the capital-output ratio $\dfrac{K}{Q}$:

$$\frac{\Delta K}{K} - \frac{\Delta Q}{Q} = (1-a) \left(\frac{\Delta K}{K} - \frac{\Delta L}{L}\right) \qquad (9)$$

Hence, if productivity is to rise, so must the capital-output ratio.

In fact, productivity has risen while the capital-output ratio has *fallen* somewhat over the past half century. What is wrong with our neoclassical model? We have omitted technical progress.

The simplest kind of technical progress to introduce is what Mrs. Joan Robinson of Cambridge calls "waving a magic wand" over the economy's inputs to make them more efficient. Suppose that this increase of efficiency yields a growth rate equal to μ independently of any increase of capital and labor. And suppose that the rate of progress μ is independent of the existing supplies of inputs. Our growth rate formula then becomes

$$\frac{\Delta Q}{Q} = \mu + a \cdot \frac{\Delta K}{K} + (1 - a) \frac{\Delta L}{L} \qquad (10)$$

And productivity increases at the rate:

$$\frac{\Delta Q}{Q} - \frac{\Delta L}{L} = \mu + a \left(\frac{\Delta K}{K} - \frac{\Delta L}{L}\right) \qquad (11)$$

Productivity growth no longer requires that capital grow faster than labor—but this helps.[5]

4. First-year calculus students ought to prove this. Others ought to think through its reasonableness: how can Q/L rise unless Q grows faster than L?

5. Also we have:

$$\frac{\Delta K}{K} - \frac{\Delta Q}{Q} = -\mu + (1 - a) \left(\frac{\Delta K}{K} - \frac{\Delta L}{L}\right) \qquad (iv)$$

The capital-output ratio can fall even though capital is growing faster than labor and thus making a contribution to productivity growth.

Thus we have two sources of productivity growth: "capital deepening" and "technical progress"—which is simply a catch-all for other sources of growth. A number of economists—Solow, Abramovitz, Kendrick and others—in the mid-Fifties, posed the following fascinating historical question: what proportion of the growth of U.S. productivity is due to the increase of capital per worker?

This proportion p is defined as the *ratio* of the growth rate of productivity which would have occurred *without* technical progress to the growth rate which actually occurred as a result of both capital deepening and technical progress. In other words, p denotes that average rate of productivity growth which is attributable to the increase in capital per manhour expressed as a *ratio* to the actual average rate of growth of productivity:

$$p = \frac{a\left(\dfrac{\Delta K}{K} - \dfrac{\Delta L}{L}\right)}{\dfrac{\Delta Q}{Q} - \dfrac{\Delta L}{L}} \tag{12}$$

It is clear immediately that if $\dfrac{\Delta K}{K} = \dfrac{\Delta Q}{Q}$ then $p = a$. How large is a, capital's relative share of GNP? Only about one-third. Moreover, since 1920 or so, $\dfrac{\Delta K}{K}$ has been smaller on average than $\dfrac{\Delta Q}{Q}$. So Solow and others concluded that *less than one-third of American productivity growth in this century can be credited to the increase in capital per worker.*

But if our investment in new capital was not awfully important in raising productivity over the past few decades, does this mean that investment would be of little use in raising productivity in the future? Not at all. It may mean simply that capital has grown very slowly in this century. Does it mean that we should have sunk all our investment resources into education and research? No, for we do not know at what enormous cost our technical progress had to be purchased.

This is the crux of the matter: Is tangible investment an ineffective or expensive way to grow? Before putting all our eggs in the research and education baskets we should investigate the prospective returns on each type of investment. But before estimating the return to tangible investment we need to note another development in the theory of capital and growth.

The Improving Quality of New Capital Goods . The unexpected
finding that investment was historically unimportant set economists to rethinking the role of capital in economic growth. It was
soon suggested that technical progress has to be embodied in
new kinds of capital goods if it is actually to raise productivity.
Therefore without continual investment productivity could not
grow at all. In this new view the role of investment is to *modernize* as well as *increase* the capital stock. It was concluded that
investment had been underrated, that it was a more effective
instrument of growth than had been thought.

Like any novel idea, this one led to exaggerations. Sometimes
more value was put on modernizing the capital stock than on
increasing it—as if modernization had made investment respectable.[6]

Granted that investment's new role as modernizing agent
makes it *more* effective. But how effective is investment? After
all, tangible investment is only one instrument of growth. Investment in research and in education are also important. Just
how attractive is an additional dollar of tangible capital formation in the U.S. economy?

The traditional measure of the attractiveness of investment is
its *net rate of return.* If capital goods never wore out and never
obsolesced as a consequence of continual improvements in the
quality of new capital goods, then the net rate of return would
be easy to figure: Under pure competition it would equal the
earnings rate on tangible capital, *i.e.*, profits as a ratio to the replacement value of the capital stock.[7]

But capital goods do depreciate and do obsolesce. So from
the gross earnings (quasirents) of capital we have to subtract
the replacement cost of the capital which wears out each year.

6. Actually a permanent modernization of the capital stock might well
be impossible—like a dog catching its tail: a massive investment in shiny
new equipment today will leave us with a massive quantity of old out-
moded equipment years hence. It is not enough to accelerate the growth of
capital for just a few years. A permanent decrease in the average age of
capital goods requires a permanent increase in the growth rate of capital.
But in the present circumstances even a temporary and short-lived modernization of the capital stock would not be unwelcome. The resulting lift
to productivity—even though temporary—could be put to good advantage.
7. A word of explanation about "replacement value": it means the
current investment cost of replacing existing productive capacity with equivalent new productive capacity. If two twenty-year-old tractors can do the
work of one two-year-old tractor, their replacement cost is the same.

And we have to subtract the decline in the replacement value of capital which is due to the ever-improving efficiency of the new capital goods with which the economy can renew and expand its capital stock. The first subtraction is called "depreciation." The second subtraction is usually called "obsolescence." Our formula for the rate of return *net* of depreciation and obsolescence is therefore

$$r = q - \delta - \iota \qquad (13)$$

where q is the gross earnings rate, δ the rate of depreciation and ι the rate of obsolescence—all measured as ratios to the replacement value of the capital stock. The rate of obsolescence as defined here is simply the rate at which new capital goods improve in efficiency.[8]

Now we can turn to the data. We select 1954 for our calculations and we restrict our attention to the business enterprise sector of the U. S. economy.

Of course, when utilization of capacity is low—as in recessions—private investors and society get very little return from their investment. We shall be concerned here with the *potential* rate of return on investment—the return that would have been received had business been good in 1954.

The Council of Economic Advisers estimates that business output that year would have been about $300 billion had there been 4% unemployment. (This concept is called "potential output.") We suppose that under these same circumstances before-tax gross earnings in the business sector would have approached $100 billion—*i.e.*, about one-third of business output.

What *gross earning rate* on tangible business capital (valued at replacement cost) would this $100 billion have yielded? Clearly this depends upon the value of the capital employed by the business sector in 1954.

The current-dollar replacement cost of the 1954 business capital stock is usually estimated at around $650 billion. (See Row 1 in the table.) But this conventional estimate neglects the quality differential between new and old capital goods: it assumes that

---

8. Advanced students may challenge the appropriateness of deducting the "improvement rate" for computation of the *social* net rate of return. This deduction is appropriate, however, for it reflects the attraction to society of waiting to invest (and advancing consumption) in order to take advantage of the future cheapening of capacity (in terms of consumption).

a 1930 truck would have to be replaced by a 1954 truck if
they had cost the same when new. But suppose the newer truck
could do the work of two old trucks. Then the true replacement
cost of a 1930 truck would be only half the cost of a new truck.

TABLE: *Potential Net Rate of Return on 1954 Business Investment*

Assumed improvement rate	Replacement cost of business capital K	Gross earnings rate q	Rate of depreciation δ	Rate of obsolescence ι	Net rate of return $q - \delta - \iota$
$\iota = 0\%$	$650 billion	15.4%	4%	0%	11.4%
$\iota = 2\%$	510 billion	19.6%	4%	2%	13.6%
$\iota = 3\%$	470 billion	21.3%	4%	3%	14.3%

NOTE: Potential gross business earnings in 1954 in the business sector
are assumed to be $100 billion.

Row 2 of the table shows a recalculation of the true replacement cost of the capital stock on the assumption that each year
there is a 2% average improvement in the efficiency of new
capital goods. Of course this estimate is lower than the conventional estimate because of the existence of "old," partially obsolete, capital in the economy.

Row 3 assumes an improvement rate of 3%. This makes the
replacement cost in terms of 1954 investment dollars still smaller.

The rest is arithmetic: Remembering to subtract an assumed
rate of depreciation of 4% and also subtracting the appropriate
assumed rate of obsolescence (improvement), we obtain three
estimates of the potential net rate of return to 1954 business investment. On the plausible assumption of 2% or 3% quality
improvement the net rate of return is estimated at about 14%.
Tangible capital need make no apologies for this respectable
rate of return.

AFTER NEOCLASSICISM

While new capital is more efficient than old capital, in the
neoclassical conception all this capital is still putty: The distinction is between (old) putty and (new) super-putty. All this
capital can be continuously and costlessly reshaped to accord
with the price of labor. As the price of labor rises over time, old

capital is supposed to be reshaped to use less labor. The labor released is then free to work with new capital.[9]

Valuable though this neoclassical conception undoubtedly is as a mental guide in many economic problems, it is also quite naïve. The typical industrial plant cannot be gradually starved of labor as neoclassical theory supposes: Instead, as the wage rate rises there must come a point where the plant must be altered and renovated if it is to be economic to produce at all. If it is not profitable to renovate, then the plant will be shut down.[10]

Economists are now developing models which capture some of these features of capital goods. A recent group of models represents a *cross* between Harrod-Domar and neoclassical ideas. Only new investments are treated as putty; once their labor requirements are decided upon, this putty turns to hard-baked clay. Thereafter this capital must be combined with labor in fixed proportions, à la Harrod-Domar.

Such models are more complex for the theorist to analyze and "ornery" for the econometrician to use in empirical studies of growth. But in time they will reward us with a better understanding of the connection between investment and growth.

9. In an efficient competitive equilibrium, labor is allocated over all "vintages" of capital in such a way that the marginal productivity of homogeneous labor will be everywhere equal.

10. Students of economics will recall that a plant will shut down if variable costs exceed revenues at the best level of production. If the plant will be economic to operate in the future, then the costs of closing down and starting up again must also be weighed in the decision to shut down temporarily.

Investment in Human Capital

THEODORE W. SCHULTZ

Theodore W. Schultz is Professor of Economics at the University of Chicago. This essay is taken from his Presidential address before the American Economic Association in December, 1960.

ALTHOUGH IT IS obvious that people acquire useful skills and knowledge, it is not obvious that these skills and knowledge are a form of capital, that this capital is in substantial part a product of deliberate investment, that it has grown in Western societies at a much faster rate than conventional (nonhuman) capital, and that its growth may well be the most distinctive feature of the economic system. It has been widely observed that increases in national output have been large compared with the increases of land, man-hours, and physical reproducible capital. Investment in human capital is probably the major explanation for this difference.

Much of what we call consumption constitutes investment in human capital. Direct expenditures on education, health, and internal migration to take advantage of better job opportunities are clear examples. Earnings foregone by mature students attending school and by workers acquiring on-the-job training are equally clear examples. Yet nowhere do these enter into our national accounts. The use of leisure time to improve skills and knowledge is widespread and it too is unrecorded. In these and similar ways the *quality* of human effort can be greatly improved and its productivity enhanced. I shall contend that such investment in human capital accounts for most of the impressive rise in the real earnings per worker.

SHYING AWAY FROM INVESTMENT IN MAN

Economists have long known that people are an important part of the wealth of nations. Measured by what labor contributes to output, the productive capacity of human beings is now vastly larger than all other forms of wealth taken together. What economists have not stressed is the simple truth that people invest in themselves and that these investments are very large. Although economists are seldom timid in entering on abstract analysis and are often proud of being impractical, they have not been bold in coming to grips with this form of investment. Whenever they come even close, they proceed gingerly as if they were stepping into deep water. No doubt there are reasons for being wary. Deep-seated moral and philosophical issues are ever present. Free men are first and foremost the end to be served by economic endeavor; they are not property or marketable assets. And not least, it has been all too convenient in marginal productivity analysis to treat labor as if it were a unique bundle of innate abilities that are wholly free of capital.

The mere thought of investment in human beings is offensive to some among us. Our values and beliefs inhibit us from looking upon human beings as capital goods, except in slavery, and this we abhor. We are not unaffected by the long struggle to rid society of indentured service and to evolve political and legal institutions to keep men free from bondage. These are achievements that we prize highly. Hence, to treat human beings as wealth that can be augmented by investment runs counter to deeply held values. It seems to reduce man once again to a mere material component, to something akin to property. And for man to look upon himself as a capital good, even if it did not impair his freedom, may seem to debase him. No less a person than J. S. Mill at one time insisted that the people of a country should not be looked upon as wealth because wealth existed only for the sake of people.[1] But surely Mill was wrong; there is nothing in the concept of human wealth contrary to his idea that it exists only for the advantage of people. By investing in themselves, people can enlarge the range of choice available to them. It is one way free men can enhance their welfare.

The failure to treat human resources explicitly as a form of capital, as a produced means of production, as the product of investment, has fostered the retention of the classical notion of labor as a capacity to do manual work requiring little knowledge and skill, a capacity with which, according to this notion, laborers

1. J. S. Nicholson, "The Living Capital of the United Kingdom," *Econ. Jour.* Mar. 1891, *1*, 95; see J. S. Mill. *Principles of Political Economy*, ed. W. J. Ashley, London, 1909, p. 8.

are endowed about equally. This notion of labor was wrong in the classical period and it is patently wrong now. Counting individuals who can and want to work and treating such a count as a measure of the quantity of an economic factor is no more meaningful than it would be to count the number of all manner of machines to determine their economic importance either as a stock of capital or as a flow of productive services.

Laborers have become capitalists not from a diffusion of the ownership of corporation stocks, as folklore would have it, but from the acquisition of knowledge and skill that have economic value.[2] This knowledge and skill are in great part the product of investment and, combined with other human investment, predominantly account for the productive superiority of the technically advanced countries. To omit them in studying economic growth is like trying to explain Soviet ideology without Marx.

ECONOMIC GROWTH FROM HUMAN CAPITAL

Many paradoxes and puzzles about our dynamic, growing economy can be resolved once human investment is taken into account. Let me begin by sketching some that are minor though not trivial.

When farm people take nonfarm jobs they earn substantially less than industrial workers of the same race, age, and sex. Similarly nonwhite urban males earn much less than white males even after allowance is made for the effects of differences in unemployment, age, city size and region. Because these differentials in earnings correspond closely to corresponding differentials in education, they strongly suggest that the one is a consequence of the other. Negroes who operate farms, whether as tenants or as owners, earn much less than whites on comparable farms.[3] Fortunately, crops and livestock are not vulnerable to the blight of discrimination. The large differences in earnings seem rather to reflect mainly the differences in health and education. Workers in the South on the average earn appreciably less than in the North or West and they also have on the average less education. Most migratory farm workers earn very little indeed by comparison with other workers. Many of them have virtually no school-

2. H. G. Johnson, "The Political Economy of Opulence," *Can. Jour. Econ. and Pol. Sci.*, Nov. 1960, *26*, 552–64.
3. Based on unpublished preliminary results obtained by Joseph Willett in his Ph.D. research at the University of Chicago.

ing, are in poor health, are unskilled, and have little ability to do useful work. To urge that the differences in the amount of human investment may explain these differences in earnings seems elementary.

Of more recent vintage are observations showing younger workers at a competitive advantage; for example, young men entering the labor force are said to have an advantage over unemployed older workers in obtaining satisfactory jobs. Most of these young people possess twelve years of school, most of the older workers six years or less. The observed advantage of these younger workers may therefore result not from inflexibilities in social security or in retirement programs, or from sociological preference of employers, but from real differences in productivity connected with one form of human investment, i.e., education. And yet another example, the curve relating income to age tends to be steeper for skilled than for unskilled persons. Investment in on-the-job training seems a likely explanation, as I shall note later.

Let me now pass on to three major perplexing questions closely connected with the riddle of economic growth. First, consider the long-period behavior of the capital-income ratio. Estimates now available show that less reproducible capital tends to be employed relative to income as economic growth proceeds. Are we to infer that the ratio of capital to income has no relevance in explaining either poverty or opulence? Or that a rise of this ratio is not a prerequisite to economic growth? These questions raise fundamental issues bearing on motives and preferences for holding wealth as well as on the motives for particular investments and the stock of capital thereby accumulated. For my purpose all that needs to be said is that these estimates of capital-income ratios refer to only a part of all capital. They exclude in particular, and most unfortunately, any human capital. Yet human capital has surely been increasing at a rate substantially greater than reproducible (nonhuman) capital. We cannot, therefore, infer from these estimates that the stock of *all* capital has been decreasing relative to income. On the contrary, if we accept the not implausible assumption that the motives and preferences of people, the technical opportunities open to them, and the uncertainty associated with economic growth during particular periods were leading people to maintain roughly a constant ratio between *all* capital and income, the decline in the estimated capital-income ratio [4] is simply a signal that human capital has been increasing relatively not only to conventional capital but also to income.

The bumper crop of estimates that show national income increasing faster than national resources raises a second and not unrelated puzzle. The income of the United States has been increasing at a much higher rate than the combined amount of land, man-hours worked and the stock of reproducible capital used to produce the income. Moreover, the discrepancy between the two rates has become larger from one business cycle to the next during recent decades. To call this discrepancy a measure of "resource productivity" [technological progress] gives a name to our ignorance but does not dispel it. If we accept these estimates, the connections between national resources and national income have become loose and tenuous over time. Unless this discrepancy can be resolved, received theory of production applied to inputs and outputs as currently measured is a toy and not a tool for studying economic growth.

Two sets of forces probably account for the discrepancy, if we neglect entirely the index number and aggregation problems that bedevil all estimates of such global aggregates as total output and total input. One is returns to scale; the second, the large improvements in the quality of inputs that have occurred but have been omitted from the input estimates. Our economy has undoubtedly been experiencing increasing returns to scale at some points offset by decreasing returns at others. If we can succeed in identifying and measuring the net gains, they may turn out to have been substantial. The improvements in the quality of inputs that have not been adequately allowed for are no doubt partly in material (nonhuman) capital. My own conception, however, is that both this defect and the omission of economies of scale are minor sources of discrepancy between the rates of growth of inputs and outputs compared to the improvements in human capacity that have been omitted.

A small step takes us from these two puzzles raised by existing estimates to a third which brings us to the heart of the matter, namely the essentially unexplained large increase in real

4. I leave aside here the difficulties inherent in identifying and measuring both the nonhuman capital and the income entering into estimates of this ratio. There are index number and aggregation problems aplenty, and not all improvements in the quality of this capital have been accounted for, as I shall note later.

earnings of workers. Can this be a windfall? It seems far more reasonable that it represents rather a return to the investment that has been made in human beings. The observed growth in productivity per unit of labor is simply a consequence of holding the unit of labor constant over time although in fact this unit of labor has been increasing as a result of a steadily growing amount of human capital per worker. As I read our record, the human capital component has become very large as a consequence of human investment.

SCOPE AND SUBSTANCE OF THESE INVESTMENTS

What are human investments? Can they be distinguished from consumption? Is it at all feasible to identify and measure them? What do they contribute to income? Granted that they seem amorphous compared to brick and mortar, and hard to get at compared to the investment accounts of corporations, they assuredly are not a fragment; they are rather like the contents of Pandora's box, full of difficulties and hope.

Human resources obviously have both quantitative and qualitative dimensions. The number of people, the proportion who enter upon useful work, and hours worked are essentially quantitative characteristics. To make my task tolerably manageable, I shall neglect these and consider only such quality components as skill, knowledge, and similar attributes that affect particular human capabilities to do productive work. In so far as expenditures to enhance such capabilities also increase the value productivity of human effort (labor), they will yield a positive rate of return.[5]

How can we estimate the magnitude of human investment? The practice followed in connection with physical capital goods is to estimate the magnitude of capital formation by expenditures made to produce the capital goods. This practice would suffice also for the formation of human capital. However, for human capital there is an additional problem that is less pressing for physical capital goods: how to distinguish between expenditures for consumption and for investment. This distinction bristles with both conceptual and practical difficulties. We can think of three

5. Even so, our *observed* return can be either negative, zero or positive because our observations are drawn from a world where there is uncertainty and imperfect knowledge and where there are windfall gains and losses and mistakes aplenty.

classes of expenditures: expenditures that satisfy consumer preferences and in no way enhance the capabilities under discussion —these represent pure consumption; expenditures that enhance capabilities and do not satisfy any preferences underlying consumption—these represent pure investment; and expenditures that have both effects. Most relevant activities clearly are in the third class, partly consumption and partly investment, which is why the task of identifying each component is so formidable and why the measurement of capital formation by expenditures is less useful for human investment than for investment in physical goods. In principle there is an alternative method for estimating human investment, namely by its yield rather than by its cost. While any capability produced by human investment becomes a part of the human agent and hence cannot be sold; it is nevertheless "in touch with the market place" by affecting the wages and salaries the human agent can earn. The resulting increase in earnings is the yield on the investment.[6]

Despite the difficulty of exact measurement at this stage of our understanding of human investment, many insights can be gained by examining some of the more important activities that improve human capabilities. I shall concentrate on five major categories: (1) health facilities and services, broadly conceived to include all expenditures that affect the life expectancy, strength and stamina, and the vigor and vitality of a people; (2) on-the-job training, including old-style apprenticeship organized by firms; (3) formally organized education at the elementary, secondary, and higher levels; (4) study programs for adults that are not organized by firms, including extension programs notably in agriculture; (5) migration of individuals and families to adjust to changing job opportunities. Except for education, not much is known about these activities that is germane here. I shall refrain from commenting on study programs for adults, although in agriculture the extension services of the several states play an important role in transmitting new knowledge and in developing skills of farmers. Nor shall I elaborate further on internal migration related to economic growth.

Health activities have both quantity and quality implications. Such speculation as economists have engaged in about the ef-

6. In principle, the value of the investment can be determined by discounting the additional future earnings it yields just as the value of a physical capital good can be determined by discounting its income stream.

fects of improvements in health,[7] has been predominantly in connection with population growth, which is to say with quantity. But surely health measures also enhance the quality of human resources. So also may additional food and better shelter, especially in underdeveloped countries.

The change in the role of food as people become richer sheds light on one of the conceptual problems already referred to. I have pointed out that extra food in some poor countries has the attribute of a "producer good." This attribute of food, however, diminishes as the consumption of food rises, and there comes a point at which any further increase in food becomes pure consumption.[8] Clothing, housing and perhaps medical services may be similar.

Surprisingly little is known about on-the-job training in modern industry. About all that can be said is that the expansion of education has not eliminated it. It seems likely, however, that some of the training formerly undertaken by firms has been discontinued and other training programs have been instituted to adjust both to the rise in the education of workers and to changes in the demands for new skills.[9] The amount invested annually in such training can only be a guess. H. F. Clark places it near to equal to the amount spent on formal education.[10] Even if it were only one-half as large, it would represent currently an annual gross

7. Health economics is in its infancy; there are two medical journals with "economics" in their titles, two bureaus for economic research in private associations (one in the American Medical and the other in the American Dental Association), and not a few studies and papers by outside scholars.

8. For instance, the income elasticity of the demand for food continues to be positive even after the point is reached where additional food no longer has the attribute of a "producer good."

9. To study on-the-job training Gary Becker [in a preliminary draft of a study undertaken in 1960 for the National Bureau of Economic Research] advances the theorem that in competitive markets employees pay all the costs of their training and none of these costs are ultimately borne by the firm. Becker points out several implications. The notion that expenditures on training by a firm generate external economies for other firms is not consistent with this theorem. The theorem also indicates one force favoring the transfer from on-the-job training to attending school. Since on-the-job training reduces the net earnings of workers at the beginning and raises them later on, this theorem also provides an explanation for the "steeper slope of the curve relating income to age," for skilled than unskilled workers, referred to earlier. Becker has also noted still another implication arising out of the fact that the income and capital investment aspects of on-the-job training are tied together, which gives rise to "permanent" and "transitory" income effects that may have substantial explanatory value.

10. Based on comments made by Harold F. Clark at the Merrill Center for Economics, summer 1959; also, see [4].

investment of about $15 billion. Elsewhere, too, it is thought to be important. For example, some observers have been impressed by the amount of such training under way in plants in the Soviet Union.[11]

Happily we reach firmer ground in regard to education. Investment in education has risen at a rapid rate and by itself may well account for a substantial part of the otherwise unexplained rise in earnings. I shall do no more than summarize some preliminary results about the total costs of education including income foregone by students, the apparent relation of these costs to consumer income and to alternative investments, the rise of the stock of education in the labor force, returns to education, and the contribution that the increase in the stock of education may have made to earnings and to national income.

It is not difficult to estimate the conventional costs of education consisting of the costs of the services of teachers, librarians, administrators, of maintaining and operating the educational plant, and interest on the capital embodied in the educational plant. It is far more difficult to estimate another component of total cost, the income foregone by students. Yet this component should be included and it is far from negligible. In the United States, for example, well over half of the costs of higher education consists of income foregone by students. As early as 1900, this income foregone accounted for about one-fourth of the total costs of elementary, secondary and higher education. By 1956, it represented over two-fifths of all costs. The rising significance of foregone income has been a major factor in the marked upward trend in the total real costs of education which, measured in current prices, increased from $400 million in 1900 to $28.7 billion in 1956. The percentage rise in educational outlays was about three and a half times as large as in consumer income, which would imply a high income elasticity of the demand for education, if education were regarded as pure consumption.[12] Educational outlays also rose about three and a half times as rapidly as did the gross formation of physical capital in dollars. If we were to treat education as pure investment this result would sug-

11. Based on observations made by a team of U. S. economists of which I was a member, see *Saturday Review*, Jan. 21, 1961.

12. Had other things stayed constant this suggests an income elasticity of 3.5. Among the things that did change, the prices of educational services rose relative to other consumer prices, perhaps offset in part by improvements in the quality of educational services.

gest that the returns to education were relatively more attractive than those to nonhuman capital.[13]

THE STOCK OF EDUCATION AND ITS RETURN

Much schooling is acquired by persons who are not treated as income earners in most economic analysis, particularly, of course, women. To analyze the effect of growth in schooling on earnings, it is therefore necessary to distinguish between the stock of education in the population and the amount in the labor force. Years of school completed are far from satisfactory as a measure because of the marked increases that have taken place in the number of days of school attendance of enrolled students and because much more of the education of workers consists of high school and higher education than formerly. My preliminary estimates suggest that the stock of education in the labor force rose about eight and a half times between 1900 and 1956, whereas the stock of reproducible capital rose four and a half times, both in 1956 prices. These estimates are, of course, subject to many qualifications. Nevertheless, both the magnitude and the rate of increase of this form of human capital have been such that they could be an important key to the riddle of economic growth.

The exciting work under way is on the return to education. In spite of the flood of high school and college graduates, the return has not become trivial. Even the lower limits of the estimates show that the return to such education has been in the neighborhood of the return to nonhuman capital. This is what most of these estimates show when they treat as costs all of the public and private expenditures on education and also the income foregone while attending school, and when they treat all of these costs as investment, allocating none to consumption.[14] But surely

13. This of course assumes among other things that the relationship between gross and net have not changed or have changed in the same proportion. Estimates are from my essay, "Education and Economic Growth" [in *Social Forces Influencing American Education*, H. G. Richey, ed., Chicago, 1961].

14. Several comments are called for here. (1) The return to high school education appears to have declined substantially between the late 'thirties and early 'fifties and since then has leveled off, perhaps even risen somewhat, indicating a rate of return toward the end of the 'fifties about as high as that to higher education. (2) The return to college education seems to have risen somewhat since the late 'thirties in spite of the rapid influx of college-

a part of these costs are consumption in the sense that education creates a form of consumer capital which has the attribute of improving the taste and the quality of consumption of students throughout the rest of their lives. If one were to allocate a substantial fraction of the total costs of this education to consumption, say one-half, this would, of course, double the observed rate of return to what would then become the investment component in education that enhances the productivity of man.

Fortunately, the problem of allocating the costs of education in the labor force between consumption and investment does not arise to plague us when we turn to the contribution that education makes to earnings and to national income because a change in allocation only alters the rate of return, not the total return. I noted at the outset that the unexplained increases in U. S. national income have been especially large in recent decades. On one set of assumptions, the unexplained part amounts to nearly three-fifths of the total increase between 1929 and 1956.[15] How

trained individuals into the labor force. (3) Becker's estimates based on the difference in income between high school and college graduates based on urban males adjusted for ability, race, unemployment and mortality show a return of 9 per cent to total college costs including both earnings foregone and conventional college costs, public and private and with none of these costs allocated to consumption. [See his study, "Underinvestment in College Education?" which follows.] (4) The returns to this education in the case of nonwhite urban males, of rural males, and of females in the labor force may have been somewhat lower (see Becker). (5) My own estimates, admittedly less complete than those of Becker and thus subject to additional qualifications, based mainly on lifetime income estimates of Herman P. Miller ["Annual and Lifetime Income in Relation to Education: 1939–1959," *Am. Econ. Review,* Dec. 1960, *50,* 962–86], lead to a return of about 11 per cent to both high school and college education as of 1958. See [Schultz, *op. cit.*]

Whether the consumption component in education will ultimately dominate, in the sense that the investment component in education will diminish as these expenditures increase and a point will be reached where additional expenditures for education will be pure consumption (a zero return on however small a part one might treat as an investment), is an interesting speculation. This may come to pass, as it has in the case of food and shelter, but that eventuality appears very remote presently in view of the prevailing investment value of education and the new demands for knowledge and skill inherent in the nature of our technical and economic progress.

15. Real income doubled, rising from $150 to $302 billion in 1956 prices. Eighty-nine billions of the increase in real income is taken to be unexplained, or about 59 per cent of the total increase. The stock of education in the labor force rose by $355 billion of which $69 billion is here allocated to the growth in the labor force to keep the per-worker stock of education constant, and $286 billion represents the increase in the level of this stock. See [Schultz, *op. cit.*] for an elaboration of the method and the relevant estimates.

much of this unexplained increase in income represents a return to education in the labor force? A lower limit suggests that about three-tenths of it, and an upper limit does not rule out that more than one-half of it came from this source.[16] These estimates also imply that between 36 and 70 per cent of the hitherto unexplained rise in the earnings of labor is explained by returns to the additional education of workers.

A CONCLUDING NOTE ON POLICY

One proceeds at his own peril in discussing social implications and policy. The conventional hedge is to camouflage one's values and to wear the mantle of academic innocence. Let me proceed unprotected!

1. Our tax laws everywhere discriminate against human capital. Although the stock of such capital has become large and even though it is obvious that human capital, like other forms of reproducible capital, depreciates, becomes obsolete, and entails maintenance, our tax laws are all but blind on these matters.

2. Human capital deteriorates when it is idle because unemployment impairs the skills that workers have acquired. Losses in earnings can be cushioned by appropriate payments but these do not keep idleness from taking its toll from human capital.

3. There are many hindrances to the free choice of professions. Racial discrimination and religious discrimination are still widespread. Professional associations and governmental bodies also hinder entry; for example, into medicine. Such purposeful interference keeps the investment in this form of human capital substantially below its optimum.[17]

4. It is indeed elementary to stress the greater imperfections of the capital market in providing funds for investment in human beings than for investment in physical goods. Much could be done to reduce these imperfections by reforms in tax and banking laws and by changes in banking practices. Long-term private and public loans to students are warranted.

5. Internal migration, notably the movement of farm people into industry, made necessary by the dynamics of our economic progress, requires substantial investments. In general, families in

16. In per cent, the lower estimate came out to 29 per cent and the upper estimate to 56 per cent.

17. Milton Friedman and Simon Kuznets, *Income from Independent Professional Practice*, National Bureau of Economic Research. New York, 1945.

which the husbands and wives are already in the late thirties cannot afford to make these investments because the remaining payoff period for them is too short. Yet society would gain if more of them would pull stakes and move because, in addition to the increase in productivity currently, the children of these families would be better located for employment when they were ready to enter the labor market. The case for making some of these investments on public account is by no means weak. Our farm programs have failed miserably these many years in not coming to grips with the costs and returns from off-farm migration.

6. The low earnings of particular people have long been a matter of public concern. Policy all too frequently concentrates only on the effects, ignoring the causes. No small part of the low earnings of many Negroes, Puerto Ricans, Mexican nationals, indigenous migratory farm workers, poor farm people and some of our older workers, reflects the failure to have invested in their health and education. Past mistakes are, of course, bygones, but for the sake of the next generation we can ill afford to continue making the same mistakes over again.

7. Is there a substantial underinvestment in human beings other than in these depressed groups? This is an important question for economists. The evidence at hand is fragmentary. Nor will the answer be easily won. There undoubtedly have been overinvestments in some skills, for example, too many locomotive firemen and engineers, too many people trained to be farmers, and too many agricultural economists! Our schools are not free of loafers and some students lack the necessary talents. Nevertheless, underinvestment in knowledge and skill, relative to the amounts invested in nonhuman capital, would appear to be the rule and not the exception for a number of reasons. The strong and increasing demands for this knowledge and skill in laborers are of fairly recent origin and it takes time to respond to them. In responding to these demands, we are heavily dependent upon cultural and political processes, and these are slow and the lags are long compared to the behavior of markets serving the formation of nonhuman capital. Where the capital market does serve human investments, it is subject to more imperfections than in financing physical capital. I have already stressed the fact that our tax laws discriminate in favor of nonhuman capital. Then, too, many individuals face serious uncertainty in assessing their innate talents when it comes to investing in themselves, especially

through higher education. Nor is it easy either for public decisions or private behavior to untangle and properly assess the consumption and the investment components. The fact that the return to high school and to higher education has been about as large as the return to conventional forms of capital when all of the costs of such education including income foregone by students are allocated to the investment component, creates a strong presumption that there has been underinvestment since, surely, much education is cultural and in that sense it is consumption. It is no wonder, in view of these circumstances, that there should be substantial underinvestment in human beings, even though we take pride, and properly so, in the support that we have given to education and to other activities that contribute to such investments.

8. Should the returns from public investment in human capital accrue to the individuals in whom it is made? [18] The policy issues implicit in this question run deep and they are full of perplexities pertaining both to resource allocation and to welfare. Physical capital that is formed by public investment is not transferred as a rule to particular individuals as a gift. It would greatly simplify the allocative process if public investment in human capital were placed on the same footing. What then is the logical basis for treating public investment in human capital differently? Presumably it turns on ideas about welfare. A strong welfare goal of our community is to reduce the unequal distribution of personal income among individuals and families. Our community has relied heavily on progressive income and inheritance taxation. Given public revenue from these sources, it may well be that public investment in human capital, notably that entering into general education, is an effective and efficient set of expenditures for attaining this goal. Let me stress, however, that the state of knowledge about these issues is woefully meager.

9. My last policy comment is on assistance to underdeveloped countries to help them achieve economic growth. Here, even more than in domestic affairs, investment in human beings is likely to be underrated and neglected. It is inherent in the intellectual climate in which leaders and spokesmen of many of these coun-

18. I am indebted to Milton Friedman for bringing this issue to the fore in his comments on an early draft of this paper. See preface of [Friedman and Kuznets, *op. cit.*] and also Jacob Mincer's pioneering paper ["Investment in Human Capital and Personal Income Distribution," *Jour. Pol. Econ.*, Aug. 1958, *66*, 281–302].

tries find themselves. Our export of growth doctrines has contributed. These typically assign the stellar role to the formation of nonhuman capital, and take as an obvious fact the superabundance of human resources. Steel mills are the real symbol of industrialization. After all, the early industrialization of England did not depend on investments in the labor force. New funds and agencies are being authorized to transfer capital for physical goods to these countries. The World Banks and our Export-Import Bank have already had much experience. Then, too, measures have been taken to pave the way for the investment of more private (nonhuman) capital abroad. This one-sided effort is under way in spite of the fact that the knowledge and skills required to take on and use efficiently the superior techniques of production, the most valuable resource that we could make available to them, is in very short supply in these underdeveloped countries. Some growth of course can be had from the increase in more conventional capital even though the labor that is available is lacking both in skill and knowledge. But the rate of growth will be seriously limited. It simply is not possible to have the fruits of a modern agriculture and the abundance of modern industry without making large investments in human beings.

Truly, the most distinctive feature of our economic system is the growth in human capital. Without it there would be only hard, manual work and poverty except for those who have income from property. There is an early morning scene in Faulkner's *Intruder in the Dust,* of a poor, solitary cultivator at work in a field. Let me paraphrase that line, "The man without skills and knowledge leaning terrifically against nothing."

Underinvestment in College Education? [1]

GARY S. BECKER

Gary S. Becker is Professor of Economics at Columbia University. This essay is taken from a paper he contributed to the annual proceedings of the American Economic Association, published in May, 1960.

IN THE LAST few years the United States has become increasingly conscious of its educational program and policies. Not only have Congress, state legislatures, and local bodies paid greater attention to this issue, but large numbers of books, articles, talks, and academic studies have also been devoted to it. This concern has been stimulated by developments in the cold war which apparently have increased the power of the Soviet Union relative to the United States. These developments are primarily the rapid economic growth of the Soviet Union in the postwar period and their obvious success in missiles and space technology.

The near panic in the United States engendered by the more spectacular Soviet accomplishments has in turn spawned a re-examination of American policies and procedures relating to economic growth and military technology. Re-examinations begot by panic almost always overestimate and overstress weaknesses and underestimate points of strength. It is perhaps not surprising, therefore, that most recent studies of American education have found it seriously deficient at all levels and in most aspects, be it the effort required, the subjects pursued, or the amount given. It is widely believed that not enough is spent on education, especially at the college and postgraduate levels, that too few of the ablest high school graduates continue their studies, that school curricula at all levels are insufficiently challenging, and that more students should be majoring in the natural sciences and engineering.

For some time now I have been conducting a study for the

1. I am indebted to A. F. Burns, S. Fabricant, Z. Griliches, J. Mincer, and T. W. Schultz for very helpful comments. Needless to say, I alone am responsible for any conclusions reached.

National Bureau of Economic Research of investment in and returns to education in the United States, especially at the college level. This study is not directly concerned with educational policy but some of the results may have relevance to the issues currently being discussed. They seem to be especially relevant in determining whether too little is spent on college education and whether the quality of our college students could be improved. This paper discusses these questions in light of the contribution of college graduates to economic growth and military technology.

The concept of economic growth used here follows that used in calculations of national income and in comparisons of the economic performance of the Soviets and the United States, and excludes, among other things, nonmonetary income. In restricting this discussion to economic growth and military technology we thus exclude the effect of education on nonmonetary returns as well as on democratic government, equality of opportunity, culture, etc. The effects on growth and technology have been greatly emphasized recently; so it is especially important to discuss them. This limitation does mean, however, that we are not attempting a complete analysis or evaluation of the effects of college expenditures. A detailed derivation of the results used here will be found in the larger study to be published by the National Bureau.

THE RATE OF RETURN ON EDUCATION

The economic effects of education can be divided into the effect on the incomes of persons receiving education and the effect on the incomes of others. This distinction largely corresponds to the distinction between private and social (i.e., external) or direct and indirect effects. Data from the last two Censuses and from other surveys giving the incomes of persons with different amounts of education make it possible to form a judgment about the direct economic effects. The Census data giving the incomes of male college and high school graduates were used to estimate the direct return to college after being adjusted for other differences between high school and college graduates, such as in ability, race, unemployment, and mortality.

The average return from college so computed is related to the average cost of college, the latter including foregone earnings or opportunity costs as well as direct college costs. Returns are related to costs by an internal rate of return—the rate of discount which equates the present value of returns and costs. In other words, it is the rate of return earned by the average college graduate on his college education. If this rate of return was significantly higher than the rate earned on tangible capital, there would be evidence of underinvestment in college education.

The rate of return relevant to a person deciding whether to go to college is a private rate, computed for private returns net of income taxes and for private costs. This was about 12½ per cent in 1940 and 10 per cent in 1950 for urban white males. The difference between these rates resulted almost entirely from the growth in the personal income tax during the forties. The rate of return in 1940, and to a lesser extent in 1950, seems large and is probably larger than the average rate earned on tangible capital. (Some evidence on this is presented shortly.)

But this is not the relevant rate in determining if there is underinvestment in education. First of all, the rate of return should be computed on total college costs, not only on those paid by students. Since in 1940 and 1950 students paid only about two-thirds of these costs, there is a considerable difference between the rates earned on private and on total costs. Second, while returns collected by the state in the form of personal income tax payments are in principle an external return, it is convenient to adjust for them now, especially since this eliminates most of the difference between the rates of return in 1940 and 1950. If then the before-tax return to college is related to the total cost of college, a rate of return of about 9 per cent is found for both 1940 and 1950. The adjustment for taxes raised the return in 1950 to about the same level as in 1940, but the adjustment for private and public subsidies to colleges reduced both rates about three percentage points. The rate of return no longer seems especially high in either year and it is an open question whether it is higher than the return on tangible capital.

Even 9 per cent is probably too high an estimate of the return to all college graduates since it refers only to urban male whites. The rate of return to nonwhites seems to be about two percentage points lower than this.[2] I made no estimates of the return to women and rural graduates and know of none made by others, but since women participate in the labor force less than men, the

2. Presumably, the difference between the return to whites and nonwhites partly results from discrimination against nonwhites.

124   GARY S. BECKER

direct money return to them is probably much less than to men.[3]
The average return to rural graduates is probably also less than
that to urban graduates. Thus the average return to all graduates would be lower than the 9 per cent return to urban white
males. That this difference might be substantial is evident, not
only from the presumed large difference in returns to urban
white males and others, but also from the fact that the former
are only about 45 per cent of all graduates.

The average return on college expenditures could be compared
to the returns on almost an endless variety of tangible capital
goods, ranging from consumers' durables to government capital.
It is easiest—and perhaps for our purposes most relevant—to
compare it to the average return on capital owned by business
enterprises. George Stigler has been preparing estimates of the
return to assets owned by manufacturing corporations. Preliminary results indicate that the rate of return on these assets, after
payment of the corporate income tax, averaged about 7 per cent,
both from 1938 to 1947 and from 1948 to 1954. This does not seem,
however, to be the relevant rate to compare with the less than
9 per cent earned on college capital which was computed *before*
the deduction of income taxes. The latter should be compared
with the return before payment of the corporate income tax.
During this period, the before-tax return of manufacturing corporations averaged more than 12 per cent of their total assets.
The data for nonmanufacturing corporations are less readily available and I do not have an estimate of the return to them. But
since corporate income tax rates were so high during this period,
it is extremely unlikely that all corporations averaged less than
10 per cent or greater than 13 per cent before taxes. Although
even less is known about unincorporated enterprises, it is unlikely
that their rate of return averaged much less than 5 per cent or
greater than 8 per cent.

The average rate of return to business capital as a whole depends on the rates of return to the corporate and unincorporated
sectors and on the relative importance of each sector. It would
appear that corporate capital is about 60 per cent of all business

3. A woman receives indirect returns from college if it enables her to
marry a man with a higher income than she would have married if she
did not go to college. These returns may be substantial and should be considered when a woman decides whether to go to college. It is not obvious
that the total return to women graduates is much less than that to men; such
a comparison would require data on the family incomes of the average male
and female college graduates rather than on their personal incomes.

capital. If this measures the relative importance of the corporate sector and if 10 and 5 per cent measure the average returns to corporate and unincorporated capital, then the average return to all business capital would be 8 per cent.

The substantial difference between these estimates and those published by others results not from difference in the basic data but in the operations performed. Most studies use private college costs rather than total costs, make no adjustment for the differential ability of college graduates, deal only with urban white or all urban males, and use a long-term interest rate to measure the rate of return elsewhere. They estimate the return to college education at about 15 per cent, and elsewhere at about 5 per cent, clearly suggesting underinvestment in college education. Using total costs reduces the rate of return on college to about 11 per cent; adjusting for differential ability reduces it further to about 9 per cent, and including nonwhites, females, and rural persons reduces it still further. On the other hand, the before-tax rate of return to business is much higher than the long-term interest rate because of risk and liquidity premiums and the heavy corporate income tax. The average rates of return to business and to college education—adjusted for these factors—do not seem very far apart.

The evidence on direct returns is limited and these estimates of direct returns subject to considerable error, but it would appear that direct returns alone cannot justify a large increase in expenditures on college education relative to expenditures on business capital. To justify large increases it is necessary to show either that improved evidence would widen the difference between the estimated returns to college and business capital or that indirect (i.e., external) returns are much larger for college than for business capital. The direct return to college was estimated from the incomes of persons differing in age and education; ideally one would like to have the lifetime incomes of persons known to differ only in education. Improvements in panel techniques and in our knowledge of the abilities of different persons may someday produce evidence close to the ideal. It remains to be seen, however, whether our conclusion about the relative returns to college and business capital is greatly changed.

External or indirect effects are very embarrassing to the economist, since his theories say little about them, he has few techniques for measuring them, and he usually does not even think that he knows much about them. In particular, little is known about the external effects from college education, although it is easy to give some examples. Thus college graduates did the pioneering work in molecular physics, and it may eventually benefit (or hurt) everyone. Einstein, Fermi, and the other pioneers received only a small fraction of the total increase (or decrease) in income resulting from their work. But it is much easier to give these examples than to assess their quantitative importance or, what is even more difficult, to compare them with external effects from business capital. Some maintain, quite persuasively, that college education had little to do with American economic growth throughout most of its history; others, equally persuasive, point to the importance of science in recent years and argue that future growth is closely related to scientific achievement; still others cite the laboratory and general increasing returns as examples of the sweeping external economies from investments in tangible capital.

Since direct returns alone do not seem to indicate underinvestment in education, those arguing this have to rely heavily on external returns. These may well be very important, but in light of our ignorance it is not surprising that no one has yet demonstrated that they are (or are not) sufficiently important to push the total return from college education much above the return elsewhere. It is this ignorance about external returns which prevents any firm judgment about the adequacy of expenditures on college education.

The Education of Scientists · Even those maintaining that external economic and military effects are important would not maintain that they are equally important in all college specialties. But there would probably be little agreement on which specialties were likely to produce these effects, and with our present knowledge it would be impossible to prove that any specialty—no matter how removed it seems from economic and military questions—was unlikely to do so. Recent discussions of the role of college education in the cold war have, however, tended to emphasize scientific specialties to the exclusion of most others, and it is possible to determine whether important external economic and military returns [4] from science alone would imply large-

4. If all persons working on military technology were employed by the government and if salaries measured expected (or actual) military contribution, there would be no external military effects since the full marginal pro-

scale underinvestment in college education.

Science majors include persons majoring in natural science, mathematics, engineering, and applied biology, and in recent years they received about one-quarter of all bachelor's and first professional degrees.[5] This is probably a large overestimate of the number likely to produce external economies. Only science majors with advanced graduate training are likely to, but less than 5 per cent of all science graduates go on for their doctorates. Scientists are more likely to produce these economies if they engage in research and development but just about 25 per cent of all scientists are so engaged. Thus it would seem that well under half of all science majors or under 13 per cent of all college graduates have a reasonable chance of producing important external economies.

It was seen that the average direct return to college graduates is about the same as the average direct return to business capital. If the direct return to scientists was no lower than the direct return to other graduates [6] and if the external military and economic effects from scientists were important, the total return to scientists would be greater than the returns to business capital. There would be underinvestment in scientists, and government assistance to the scientific field would be required to attain a more optimal allocation of capital. The number of scientists would be increased partly at the expense of business investment, partly at the expense of current consumption, and perhaps partly at the expense of other professions.

The important point to note, however, is that even a large underinvestment in scientists implies only a small underinvest-

---

ductivity would be directly measured by salaries. This argument clearly holds for all government employees regardless of their specialty.

5. Business had about 14 per cent, education about 20 per cent, and humanities and social sciences about 25 per cent of all first degrees.

6. Few systematic studies have been made of the return to different college specialties. According to the 1950 Census the average income of engineers was about $5,100, much lower than the $6,600 average income of college graduates. This seems to indicate that the direct money return to engineering graduates is less than that to other graduates. But about 40 per cent of the Census engineers are not college graduates, and they may receive less income than graduate engineers simply because they have less training. Moreover, even if they have the same total amount of training—received on the job rather than in college—they would tend to report lower incomes because their incomes would be net of training costs, while the reported incomes of graduate engineers (and other college graduates) would be gross of training costs.

ment in college education as a whole. For example, the number of scientists with prospects of producing external effects could be increased by as much as 50 per cent—a very sizable increase—and yet less than a 7 per cent increase in the total number of college graduates would be required. The 7 per cent figure is arrived at by assuming that none of the increase in scientists is at the expense of other college specialties and that a full 13 per cent of all graduates fall into the relevant "scientist" category. Even 7 per cent must, therefore, be considered a liberal upper estimate. So the current demand for a large increase in scientists (or, more generally, expenditures on scientific training) to stimulate development could be met with a very modest increase in total expenditures on college education. This does not mean that underinvestment in scientists is unimportant, but only that it could be corrected with a relatively small expenditure.

Let me conclude by briefly summarizing the discussion. Several aspects of college education in the United States were examined in terms of their contribution to economic and military progress. The limited available evidence did not reveal any significant discrepancy between the direct returns to college education and business capital, and thus direct returns alone do not seem to justify increased college expenditures. This puts the burden on external or indirect returns since they would have to be important to justify increased expenditures. Unfortunately, very little is known about them; so a firm judgment about the extent of underinvestment in college education is not possible.

Many recent discussions have emphasized the external contributions of scientists to economic and military progress and have called for large increases in scientific personnel. Such an increase could be accomplished with a small increase in total college expenditures. A large increase in expenditures would be warranted only if external returns were produced by a much larger fraction of all college graduates.

Research and Economic Growth:
The Role of Public Policy

BENTON F. MASSELL AND RICHARD R. NELSON

Benton F. Massell and Richard R. Nelson are economists at the RAND Corporation. RAND engages in research related to matters of national security. This article first appeared in the Winter 1962 California Management Review.

SINCE HAMILTON's first report on manufactures, this country has not let decisions affecting economic growth be made exclusively by private individuals and groups. Our tariff history, the patent laws, the homestead act, the land grants to railroads, the establishment of numerous government agencies to help private industry prosper and grow, the public development of land and water resources in many areas, public support of education and research —all these testify to the large role that public agencies have played in our growth.

But those who argue that economic growth is a useful means to several desired ends should be well aware of the fact that there are other and alternative means. For example, rapid economic growth is essential to the maintenance of full employment only to the extent that we let investment take much of the burden of providing aggregate demand. We could aim for a higher level of consumption and of government services, in which case investment would be a less important source of demand, and the amount of economic growth needed to call forth that investment would be significantly smaller. The authors, though strong advocates of economic growth both as an end in itself and as a means to other ends, are concerned lest alternative and complementary policies to these other ends may tend to get lost in the din of growthmanship.

In our economy the government sector spends about one-fifth of Gross National Product, taxes take an equal share, the operations of the Treasury and the Federal Reserve Board comprise a significant fraction of our total transactions in paper assets, and government debt is a major portion of total debt outstanding. The everyday fiscal and monetary operations of the government thus have a significant impact on investment and, consequently, on economic growth.

Over half of our Research and Development is government financed, and though the objective of the bulk of this program is improved defense, it obviously affects the rate of economic progress. In these areas, and in many others, government policies do affect our economic growth rate, and in an important way. The real question, though, is, should the government consciously pursue a set of policies *expressly designed* to step up the growth rate? And, if so, what sorts of measures are called for?

We think that one promising avenue to explore is an expanded government participation in our research effort. In recent years, economists have begun to realize that technological progress is a key to rapid economic growth. As scientific research is an important element in the creation of technological change, policies aimed at stimulating various areas of science may be useful instruments of a national growth policy.

Economic Progress and Technical Change · Atomic energy, modern drugs, plastics, electronic computers, synthetic fibers— these products, which have resulted directly from twentieth-century science, should make us aware of the great role that invention has played in our economic progress. Scientific research enters the picture by creating the knowledge which permits us to develop these new and improved products and processes.

Perhaps, therefore, we can gain a better understanding of the importance of research by attempting to gauge the contribution of technical change to our economic progress. The resulting measure will be crude. Much technical progress is independent of research, and, moreover, sometimes research contributes to economic progress by routes other than that of creating technical change. Nevertheless, measuring the relative importance of technical change will provide us with a better notion of the significance of research.

Let us use increase in per worker productivity as an index of economic progress. In order to isolate the contribution of technological change, we must separate this factor from other factors which contribute to increased productivity: (1) Greater use of capital equipment per worker, or what the economist terms "capital deepening," (2) more efficient allocation of resources in firms, and among firms and industries, and (3) increase in the level of education and skill of both labor and management.

A recent study by one of the authors suggests that between 30 percent and 40 percent of the past increase in output per worker was accounted for by capital deepening and improved resource allocation. Consequently, at least 60 percent must be explained by technical change and improved working force quality. Similar studies by other economists and statisticians have tended to support these conclusions. Thus, education and technical change emerge as potent economic forces.

Of course these statistical results must be qualified by the existence of interactions among the four sets of factors. For example, changes in technology frequently need to be incorporated in new capital goods before becoming effective. Thus it would be wrong to use the importance of technical change as an argument for abandoning investment activity.

Nevertheless, the results of these statistical procedures are illustrative of the major role which technical change has played. Moreover, these results are supported by other, more direct, evidence of the importance of research. Technical change starts with invention, and there is convincing evidence that science is playing an increasingly instrumental role in inventive activity.

Patent statistics, research and development expenditure data, and counts of "important inventions" have all recently been used in attempts to measure the rate of invention and the level of inventive activity in various industries and sectors of the economy. The data reveal a secular shift in inventive activity away from industries based on craft and simple mechanical engineering, and toward industries based on modern chemistry and physics—in other words, toward those industries where science is important. The data also suggest a growing importance of the industrial research and development laboratory—the modern institution harnessing science to technical progress.

As one would expect, there is a significant correlation between the amount of research and development work a firm does and the number of significant inventions accredited to it. And the firms which do a lot of inventing tend to grow faster, and be more profitable.

Additional indirect evidence of the contribution of research is provided by studies of the returns earned by investment in research and development. The studies which have been done are of success stories, but the figures they suggest are remarkably high, even granting this source of bias. For example, the research which led to hybrid corn has yielded returns of several hundred percent a year. And calculations made by some of the larger industrial laboratories also suggest rates of return to research well above profits earned from investment in plant and equipment.

One study, attempting to measure directly the impact of research on productivity, and on the technological change component of productivity increase, showed that the firms of an industry which do the most research and development tend to have the most rapid rate of technological change; and the industries where productivity is growing the fastest have typically been the research-intensive industries.

RESEARCH AS INVESTMENT IN KNOWLEDGE

How does research contribute to technical change? In one sense, by increasing and enriching our stock of knowledge. There are many difficulties connected with defining the stock of knowledge. Certainly it involves much more than formal scientific knowledge, and research is by no means the sole activity by which knowledge is increased. Indeed, writers who use as their examples the inventions of the 18th and 19th centuries have tended to argue that formal scientific knowledge is unimportant to inventors—what is important is general technological know-how.

However, writers who have used as their examples the more recent advances in chemical and electronic technology have argued that, though formal science may not have been particularly important in the more distant past, it has played a more major role in recent inventive activity.

The stock of knowledge may play a permissive role or a triggering role. In its permissive role the stock of knowledge and changes in it acts primarily through its effect on the costs of solving already perceived practical problems. Knowledge serves primarily as a reference book determining the skill with which people concerned with solving practical problems are able to surmount the difficulties. Where knowledge plays this permissive role, the evidence is that demand, or social need, is the primary factor determining what problems people try to solve, and the stock of knowledge determines how, and with what success, they go about solving them.

In some industries, the stock of knowledge has played a more active role, and advances in scientific knowledge have served to trigger inventive activity. That is, advances in knowledge have generated searches for problems the knowledge could be applied to. This seems to be the case with a number of advances in chemical technology and in electronics.

It is useful to treat both fundamental scientific research and the more applied forms of inventive activity as part of a spectrum of activities aimed at increasing our stock of technical knowledge. At one end of the spectrum is fundamental research, at the other end practical engineering and inventing. Moving from the pure science end of the spectrum to the engineering end, the goals become more clearly defined in terms of specific practical problems; the predictability of the results tends to increase; the chances that the results will be directly of use increases; and the chances of patenting improve.

There are some important implications of this. Though knowledge is always a difficult commodity to buy and sell on a market, the chances that a company will be able to capture on the market a good share of the benefits created by the research and development it undertakes are much greater toward the engineering end of the spectrum than toward the basic science end of the spectrum. For this reason, profit incentives work a good deal better in applied research and development than in fundamental research. It is important to keep this point in mind—it is of major importance in designing effective public policy.

Government's Role in Research · The actions of the federal government already impinge on scientific research in a vast number of areas, in many different ways, and for a wide diversity of reasons. In some cases, the responsibilities of the federal government are almost accidental. The Smithsonian Institute is under the jurisdiction of our government because long ago a wealthy

Englishman admired American democracy. In many cases, the original problems which led the government into an area of science have long disappeared. But perhaps the main reasons why the government has become involved in science are the following:

First, we have the concern with certain areas of science derived from problems of managing efficiently those sectors of our political economy where we have established public, as contrasted with private, decision-making organizations. Examples of this type of interest are defense, research to improve public health, weather forecasting, and geographical surveys. These all have in common the fact that the goods and services involved are public goods.

Second, fundamental scientific knowledge itself can be considered a public good, for the total benefits which accrue from a fundamental scientific advance exceed those which can be traded on the free market. In recent years, the Federal government has acted to sponsor research in certain key areas, such as peacetime atomic energy and space technology, on the grounds that the advances which might result would be sufficiently widespread in their impact to be treated as public goods.

A third, and more restricted, reason for federal involvement has been the existence of a number of industries and sectors in which, though nonresearch decisions are largely made by private organizations, it is felt that public interest in advancing technology surpasses the interests or capabilities of the private organizations involved. Agriculture, civil aviation, and the work of the National Bureau of Standards are examples of this interest.

We are suggesting a fourth reason for federal encouragement of science and technology—to stimulate economic growth.

PUBLIC POLICY TOWARD RESEARCH

One of the main tasks of policy formation is to decide which areas of science can be financed and managed by nongovernmental organizations in such a way as to lead to socially satisfactory results, and which areas need the financial support, and perhaps the direction of governmental agencies. In the United States, we have developed a satisfactory division of labor between public and private agencies, between agencies whose goals are the general welfare and organizations whose goals are those of the controlling individuals. We have thus achieved decentralization and flexibility with only a relatively small degree of discord and coordination failure.

This division of labor has worked so well principally because of a correlated set of institutions which have tended to make private incentives reflect the social interest. It is important to keep this division of labor within our scientific institutions, and this means two things. First, where the public interest is reasonably well reflected in private profit opportunities, we should continue to rely on private groups to do the job. Second, in those areas where private incentives and the public interest are not in accord, we should take steps either to bring them into accord or to get the job done through public agencies.

In addition to selecting areas where governmental action is desirable, the formulation of effective policy depends upon the choice of appropriate policy instruments. The instruments of public policy toward science are many and varied. Consider, for example, the following: government establishment and administration of research laboratories; special public agencies which contract for private research; the provision of relatively untied research funds; and various laws and institutions which can influence and aid private institutions in undertaking research. Government policy is synonymous neither with government decision making nor with government funding.

How Good Is Industrial Research? · Direct subsidization of private industrial research should be the least important aspect of our over-all policies to accelerate growth by stimulating science. There is some room for useful change in our tax, patent, and industrial organization laws. And the whole area of patent rights on government financed research needs rethinking. Indeed, perhaps we should reconsider the entire patent system.

But it seems likely that in the type of work done by industrial laboratories there is a smaller gap between public benefit and private incentives than in any other area of research and development. And, given that our over-all scientific resources are limited (as is government ability to formulate and manage policy effectively), the industrial research laboratory does not appear to need immediate government attention. Though direct public support of industrial research does not seem a wise move, there may be significant gains from public policies designed to strengthen the link between scientific knowledge and research and development.

The preponderance of the work done in industrial research laboratories is not scientific research as it has been defined in this paper, and as it is traditionally defined. Most of it is problem solving, and development and design work, involving little or no effort to achieve a greater understanding of underlying physical principles. Although industrial research and development draws heavily on science, it does not contribute much to science.

There are good reasons why this is so; why the research groups at the Bell Telephone Laboratories, General Electric, and a few other companies are the exceptions, not the rule. The results of fundamental research are quite unpredictable. At the outset of a fundamental research effort it is very difficult to predict with any real precision just what practical problems will be illuminated as a result of the research. Only companies operating on a very broad technological base and producing a wide range of products can have any real confidence that the applied areas which are illuminated are areas of immediate interest to them.

Further, the way that advances in fundamental knowledge yield practical advances is usually extremely diffuse. Cases like the transistor and nylon, where the results of laboratory research led directly to the invention of new products, are rare. Indeed, many of the companies that maintain fundamental research groups do not consider the principal role of these groups to be the creation of knowledge the companies can use. Rather, these groups are seen as the windows through which the company views the general world of science.

It is the primary job of these groups to keep the company, and in particular the applied research and development people, aware of scientific knowledge, new and old, which can be used profitably in the development of new products and processes. For very rarely do specific advances in science yield specific advances in technology. More generally, a particular technical advance clothes a number of applied scientific principles, some new, most of them old.

Thus if we separate scientific research from invention and development, we cannot expect profit-oriented companies to play a major role in our research effort. Some companies in some industries will find scientific research profitable. But in only a few of the giant companies, with a great range of diversified products, is real research a paying proposition, if the direct benefits of in-house research are considered alone.

The main contribution of the groups in industry doing fundamental research is the excellent contact with the general world of science which they provide. However, fundamental research groups are expensive to maintain. Many companies are not sufficiently large to make it profitable for them to keep a staff of good scientists whose main function is to keep the company abreast of developments.

In a number of industries, no company is of sufficient size, or diversity of product line and technology, for a fundamental research group to be profitable. This suggests that it may be promising to do more experimentation with industry-wide research organizations. And the support and encouragement of these organizations may be a legitimate function of government.

In those industries where production techniques and market structure tend to lead to firms of small size, and in those industries which are characterized by the dominance of mature firms with no research tradition, there may be significant payoffs from sponsoring cooperative research institutions which stress relatively fundamental work on the sciences that underlie the industries' technology. The main function of these institutions should be the closer linking of the industry with science.

Government Aid for Basic Research · While cooperative research laboratories may have a positive contribution to make, policies aimed at stimulating fundamental science, improving the efficiency of the over-all scientific effort, and, over the long run, increasing our supply of trained scientists and engineers should be the core of our policy. For it is in just these areas that private financing is most inadequate to serve the public's needs. Fundamental research has all of the characteristics of an activity where public benefits exceed private profit opportunities.

Because public support of fundamental research need not imply direct governmental controls of any major sort, policies in this area have the advantage of not extending the area of direct governmental decision making in our society. Further, since the recipients of government support would be, by and large, nonprofit organizations, the economic and political pressures—and the consequent conflict of interest—are relatively small. Nor are there major problems of public control and private incentives which tend to arise when government-supported research in a profit-oriented laboratory results in something of significant commercial worth.

However, an effective public policy must be formulated in awareness of the way that fundamental research contributes to economic progress. As we have seen, the results are unpredictable and, if planning is used in a tight sense, unplannable. Obtaining results from basic research is not like getting candy from a slot machine.

The organization of fundamental science reflects this fact. Within basic science the allocation of effort is determined in part by the interests of individual scientists, in part by the professional judgment of an elite who have considerable control over resources and rewards, and in part by incentives and funds provided by organizations interested in research in certain areas.

The first two factors tend to cause research resources to be shifted toward areas which seem ripe for new discoveries, where ripeness is usually signaled by interesting goings-on. The third factor tends to draw scientific resources toward areas where certain practical payoffs are perceived.

There are two broad questions of social policy raised here. One is the extent to which considerations other than those of scientific interest should influence the allocation of research resources. The evidence is reasonably clear that really major advances in knowledge are more likely to come when scientists are able to follow their own interests, than when scientists are constrained to work in fields where certain immediate payoffs are expected.

On the other hand, it is important that research be done in areas where success is likely to be socially, politically, or economically important. An enlarged Federal role in the support of basic research, if it is to be effective, clearly must strike a balance between these two considerations.

A successful basic research program is heavily dependent upon the quality of our educational system; support of scientific and technical education may well be the most effective long-run policy for stimulating economic progress. People with scientific training are needed not only to do research and development work. They are needed in many other functions. Indeed, less than one-third of our engineers and scientists are engaged in research and development.

Technically trained people are needed in production management, in sales, in administrative positions of all sorts, and in top management. One of the more important roles of the scientist in management, not actively doing research and development, is as a sympathetic and critical appraiser of the new ideas which come out of the labs. The non-research-and-development scientist and engineer is a vital link between invention and innovation.

Encouraging Major Breakthroughs · Another extremely promising area of Federal policy lies in helping the development of major new technological breakthroughs. Atomic energy and space have set the precedent here. The decision to establish a quasi-governmental agency to sponsor and play a major role in developing the peacetime atomic energy industry represented a significant, if not unprecedented, break with tradition. (A similar decision had been made in the 1920s with respect to aviation when the NACA was established.)

One significant reason for this decision was that the risks and costs of the major research effort considered necessary for a satisfactory rate of progress seemed larger than those which private companies would be willing to undertake by themselves. Research relating to the introduction of major new technologies, by its very nature, offers a small probability of a tremendous gain and a large probability of no gain at all. Some sort of risk-sharing and profit-sharing scheme is consequently called for. The result of such a scheme may well be to tilt the risk-gain scale in such a way as to create incentives for research in areas which were previously regarded as unprofitable.

The establishment of the National Aeronautics and Space Administration to direct our research on peacetime uses of space technology reflects these considerations. It appears likely that modern science will open up new technological fields with similar characteristics in the future; and if public agencies aren't established to explore these fields, we may fail to devote sufficient scientific resources to them.

At the present stage of our knowledge, it is nonsense to talk about such things as an "optimum" research effort in anything but a highly theoretical manner. Perhaps some day our knowledge of the way that research contributes to economic growth will be sufficiently sound to enable quite precise predictions of the impact of various policies to be made. But at the present the best strategy is to be flexible and experimental.

We are convinced that policy toward science should recognize the division of labor between governmental and private units, and focus on those areas of science where the evidence is clearest that private incentives do not reflect adequately the public interest.

These areas include almost all of fundamental research, the whole field of scientific education, major and costly research efforts that are likely to open up new areas of technology, and perhaps industry research of the sort which will enable firms which cannot afford to support research to gain closer links with the world of science. Because the public interest is better reflected by profit opportunities in the applied fields, where there is a well established industrial research structure, the gains from increased public support in this area seem much less than in the areas marked out above.

The gains from public attention to these issues are potentially vast. Hopefully, by mobilizing our scientific resources, we can accelerate the rate of growth in economic activity sufficiently to meet the Soviet challenge.

Can There Be Too Much Research?

FRITZ MACHLUP

Fritz Machlup is Professor of Economics at Princeton University. This article first appeared in Science. *It is part of a series of papers emerging from the author's study of the economics of knowledge.*

THIS ARTICLE deals with an important question arising from the recent growth of research and development and the loud cheers that have accompanied this growth. Several kinds of research will be touched upon, but my chief subject will be industrial research and development. This four-word phrase will be referred to often, and the use of "IRAD" as a code word for it will save space.

PHENOMENAL GROWTH OF IRAD

It has been estimated that the expenditures for IRAD in 1930 were less than $120 million; in 1953 they were $3700 million, and in 1956 they were $6500 million. One might make two reservations concerning the legitimacy of measuring the growth of IRAD by dollar outlays: that the data for the earlier years are not reliable and that the value of the dollar has diminished over the period. Yet neither of these considerations can throw any doubt on the order of magnitude of the figures in question.

The figures for recent years include large amounts of public funds spent by industry under government contracts; in 1956 no less than 49 percent came from the Federal Government. In addition there were direct expenditures of the Government for research and development performed by its own agencies ($1400 million) and expenditures for research, basic and applied, in universities and other nonprofit institutions. Some expenditures for *basic* scientific research are included in the figures for IRAD, but this is only a small portion—about 5 percent in 1953—of the

141

activities of industrial organizations. Hence, when we speak of IRAD we mean primarily *applied* research and development, designed to produce new or improved technology—some of it in the form of inventions, patentable or unpatentable; some of it concerned with the application or adaptation of inventions and the acquisition of know-how; but all of it useful in industrial production involving new products, new devices, new processes.

Much of the phenomenal growth of IRAD has been connected with the war and defense effort of the nation, either directly, as in the execution of "crash programs" for the development of weapons and other defense materiel, or indirectly through the transfer of the "research-mindedness" of defense production to industry in general. Some of the increase in IRAD expenditures has probably been connected with the tax laws, especially the combination of high corporate income tax rates (and still higher excess-profits tax rates after the war) with the deductibility of IRAD payrolls from taxable income. In any case, industrial research has become very popular, not only among industrialists but also with the consuming public, as one can infer from the public-relations emphasis upon industrial research. In the main, the new research-mindedness of industry has probably proved profitable as well as productive, and everybody is satisfied that the increase in industrial research has been a splendid thing all around.

THE MORE THE BETTER?

If this past increase has been such a desirable development, should we be content with the level attained or should we press for more? Should we devote an ever-increasing portion of our resources (chiefly human resources) to industrial research, or is there perhaps some limit beyond which we should not go? It is easy to see that an economy might fail to allocate enough of its resources to IRAD. But can there ever be too much? Is not more research and development always better than less?

For most noneconomists the answer looks simple: More IRAD will produce more invention of better products and of better production techniques; this, in turn, will raise our standard of living; hence, we should always encourage industrial research, by allotting more government funds, by further liberalizing the tax laws, by strengthening the patent system, by employing whatever methods seem appropriate. "Let us have more IRAD, the more the better."

This view fails to recognize the existence of an economic problem—that is, a problem of choosing among alternatives. Economics comes in where more of one thing means less of another. To be sure, it would be nice to have more of a good thing, but if this implies that there will be less of something else, one should compare and choose. It is the economist's task to analyze what alternatives society will have to forego when it does what seems so desirable to many or to all. The social cost of what *is* done is the value of what *might* be done instead. In technical terms, the social cost of any action is equal to the value of the most valuable alternative opportunity that has to be foregone.

Many highly sophisticated economists will likewise incline to the view that there should be more inventive activity, not because it would be without social cost, but because the social cost is apt to be much smaller than the social benefit from the increased activity. They are convinced that society stands to gain from a shift of resources toward "inventing." By and large, economists in the free world are willing to rely on the price mechanism to guide or steer resources into the most wanted uses. But they recognize that there are certain situations or areas in which market prices and business profits will not adequately reflect the social benefits derived from particular goods or services. The private benefits that can be derived from inventive work are, as a rule, less than the potential social benefits. To express it in the economists' lingo: Since the "external benefits" of inventions —"external" because they accrue to individuals other than their producers and users—are substantial, the "social marginal product" of inventive activity is greater than the "private marginal product"; this implies that without government intervention not enough resources are allocated to the business of inventing, and that the total social product—the flow of real output—could be increased by shifting additional resources to IRAD.

WHENCE THE MANPOWER?

From what sectors of the economy can one withdraw the productive resources that are to be transferred to IRAD? Let us list all conceivable "sectors" that might be raided for manpower and then ask how likely each of them is to give up the human resources wanted for increased IRAD. (There are also IRAD expenditures for resources other than human, but the problems of finding buildings, apparatus, and materials needed for IRAD are not so serious.) "Inventive personnel" may be recruited by getting qualified persons away from (i) involuntary leisure, (ii) voluntary leisure, (iii) the production of security from invasion and revolution (including the production of military goods), (iv) the production of consumers' goods, (v) the production of capital goods, (vi) basic research, or (vii) education.

A shift of qualified persons from "involuntary leisure" to inventive activities would surely be the best of all possibilities, since the diminution of involuntary idleness would be a boon rather than a sacrifice. It would mean that there have been unemployed talents waiting to be used—talented individuals anxious to give up the leisure that had been imposed on them. This possibility, however, must be written off as an illusion if we are engaged in serious economic analysis. "Depression economics," based on the assumption that there are pools of unemployed resources ready to be put to work, has its uses, but only for what has been called an "upside-down economy." Economic theory and economic policy for the "right-side-up economy" would be badly vitiated by the assumption that there are ever-ready pools of productive resources that can be drawn upon at any time, to any extent, for any use.

A shift from "voluntary leisure" would be the next best possibility. It would mean that some qualified people are ready, with some inducements, to devote more time to inventive activity, not at the expense of any other productive activity but at the expense of some of their leisure time. These people may be professionals or amateurs. The former are the scientists and engineers already in IRAD and possibly willing to work overtime. This pool of potential resources may be of great importance for the implementation of "crash programs" of research and development in a national emergency. But long-run programs, not directed toward specific goals (like winning a war or an international race for accomplishment of a particular technical feat) but designed for "progress in general," cannot successfully be based on the continuous and continual supply of overtime labor. The other source of volunteer labor—amateur researchers and tinkerers, busy with other jobs during their regular hours but glad to use their free evenings and weekends for inventive activity—can probably be drawn upon regularly. (Mobilization of these "individual inventors" was perhaps one of the achievements of the patent system in times past.) But this is a very limited source of supply, perhaps already fully utilized; in addition, the role of the "evening-and-Sunday inventors" has become quite insignificant in our age of organized research and development. Thus, the possible sacrifice of leisure cannot be counted on to provide the labor for additional inventive activity.

One must assume that society has allocated to national defense the resources that its experts consider indispensable. If the threat of invasion or revolution increases, resources will have to be withdrawn from other uses; if that threat is reduced, resources can be transferred and larger allocations can be made elsewhere. But one cannot reasonably assume that civilian industry, when it wants to increase its IRAD staff, will be able to raid the defense establishment or defense production for large numbers of engineers, even if one could find there the men qualified to do inventive work.

ALTERNATIVE OR COMPLEMENTARY GROWTH?

Having disposed of—as illusory—the first three hypothetical pools of manpower for additions to the IRAD staff, we may find it expedient to stop a moment for reorientation. The sectors left for consideration are the production of consumers' goods, the production of capital goods, basic research, and education. Let us now combine basic research, education, and applied research and development (including IRAD) into one sector, called "production of knowledge," and examine its relation to the other two. Is it really correct to regard these three sectors of production as alternatives? Since they actually have grown together, should they not rather be considered as complementary? Has not every increase in the production of capital goods helped, rather than hindered, the growth in the production of consumers' goods? Has not every increase in the production of knowledge accelerated, rather than retarded, the growth in the production of both capital goods and consumers' goods? Evidently, here is a conflict in economic interpretation that must be resolved before we can proceed.

Historically, production has increased simultaneously in all three areas; looking back over long periods, one does not find any absolute reduction in the production of consumers' goods when more resources were allocated to the production of capital equipment and of knowledge. Simultaneous increases in all areas have been possible because of the increase in the total labor force and because of the advance of productivity. As more manpower became available, absolutely larger numbers could be allocated to all lines of endeavor; an increased allocation to one sector did not presuppose an absolute curtailment of others. But in percentage terms the allocation was still a matter of alternatives. And it is in these terms, and in terms of output per head, that the problem of resource allocation in an economy with rising population must be analyzed. Clearly, a relative increase in the allocation of resources to any one line of endeavor implies relative curtailments of others.

Even with a constant labor force it is possible for production in all areas to increase if productivity—output per worker—increases. And productivity will almost certainly increase as more capital equipment and more technical knowledge are accumulated. Hence, with the advance of productivity it becomes possible to reduce the allocation of resources to the production of consumers' goods, and to increase the allocation to other areas, without causing any decline in final output. Indeed, this gradual reallocation of resources from consumers' goods production to the accumulation of capital and of knowledge will cause the output of consumers' goods, in the long run, to increase even faster.

This does not contradict the truth about the fundamental "alternativeness" of production of consumers' goods, capital equipment, and knowledge. At any moment of time, the three "departments of production" compete for the available resources, and increases in the allocations to the production of capital and knowledge at a rate faster than the rate of growth of manpower and of productivity will reduce the per capita output of consumers' goods in the near future.

COMPETITION FOR SCARCE RESOURCES

The notion that an increase in the production of capital goods or in the production of knowledge should, if only temporarily, hold back the production of consumers' goods is so contrary to widespread preconceptions that we must not expect it to be easily accepted. Some slightly more thorough elaboration, or even a repetitive reformulation, may therefore be appropriate, or at least forgivable.

An increase in the stock of knowledge may lead to a rise in productivity and thus to increases in the output of consumers' goods and capital goods. Similarly, an increase in the stock of capital goods may raise productivity and thus permit increases in production. This may suggest that the most rapid accumulation of capital goods and knowledge will permit the fastest increase in consumption. But, alas, such accumulation presupposes the availability of resources. If resources are being fully used, increased appropriations for investment in capital and knowledge must imply reduced appropriations to the production of consumers' goods. There is, therefore, a dilemma: The way to increase consumption is first to reduce it. Only by reducing the production of consumers' goods can society transfer resources to the production of capital goods and useful knowledge, and only subsequently can the increased stocks of capital and knowledge raise productivity enough to enable the diminished resources that are allotted to consumers' goods production to bring their output back to the former level and above it.

Increased research and development in order to increase the stock of knowledge is a splendid thing for society; so is increased production of productive equipment, and both are so highly valued because they eventually allow increased consumption. Yet, these three—more knowledge, more equipment, and more consumption—are alternatives in the sense that, even though all three can increase when productivity increases, a greater increase of one must mean, for the time being, smaller increases of the others. At any one moment, an increase in the production of knowledge means less equipment or less consumption than might otherwise be available, or less of both. A choice by society to increase research and teaching implies a choice, though usually unconscious, to have in the next years less productive equipment or less consumption, or less of both, than they might have had. Should a relative cutback of consumption prove impracticable, the choice is between "knowledge" and "equipment."

The Choice Between Research and Education · If resources are shifted from education to IRAD, the accumulation of new technical knowledge may be accelerated at the expense of the dissemination of established general knowledge. It is possible for industry, by providing more attractive job opportunities (for IRAD as well as for other kinds of qualified work), to drain schools of the teachers needed for the instruction of the new generation. The time may come when a lack of adequately trained graduates of the schools creates a bottleneck, obstructing not only further progress in the arts but also the maintenance of the general productivity of the people.

As in the formation and reproduction of capital, the problem is one of timing. Pushing IRAD *now*, in order to increase the production of new technical knowledge, may be at the expense of the reproduction of established knowledge and may result in an eventual decrease of general productivity with a forced reduction of IRAD *later*, perhaps even with a net loss in the production of technical knowledge in the long run.

BASIC AND APPLIED RESEARCH

It has been customary to divide knowledge, teaching, and research into two main categories, one of which is characterized as general, fundamental, liberal, basic; the other, as applied, practical, vocational, technical. The distinction is a useful one, even if blurred in many instances. The difference between basic and applied research happens to be significant for our present inquiry: whether there can be too much research.

We have stated that IRAD competes for the kind of human resources that are required for educating the young. Schoolteaching and applied research are largely alternative occupations. The instances in which a man in IRAD work also teaches an evening class, or in which a teacher also serves as an industrial consultant, are merely exceptions which confirm the rule that applied research and teaching are alternatives. This is not the case with basic research, which to some extent is a complementary activity of teachers at advanced levels.

The essential complementarity between teaching (especially postgraduate) and basic research has always been recognized by institutions of higher education. The performance of university professors is judged, as a rule, by their research work, and it is from the great research scholars that advanced students have received their most lasting inspirations. Of course, teaching and research cannot be complementary where heavy teaching loads make it impossible for college teachers to carry on any significant research. Perhaps, if the amount of teaching is measured by the hours of classroom work, all research must be considered an alternative to teaching; only when the amount of teaching is measured by the results achieved—in terms of the intellectual capacities developed—will basic research be recognized as complementary to teaching on the highest levels.

The social benefits of basic research are invaluable, and its social cost is probably not too high. For apparently only a relatively small number of people can qualify as workers in basic research, and, hence, the promotion of basic research will not encroach heavily on other pursuits. If those who do basic research are engaged in higher education, their usefulness as teachers may be increased, not diminished. And when the funds for basic research go to institutions of higher education, such outlays stimulate the employment not only of better but also of *more* academic teachers by enabling universities to meet more successfully the attractive salaries industry offers to qualified scholars in administrative posts and IRAD positions. In other words, increased public outlays for basic research are not likely to encroach on education. On the contrary, they may aid education by allowing universities to hold on to scholars who might otherwise be lured into industry, by allowing scholars to improve their qualifications as teachers, and by attracting more qualified young people into careers of scholarship. On these grounds one may say that there is little danger of there being "too much basic research."

IRAD AND ADEQUATE EDUCATION

However, IRAD and education—the acquisition of new applied knowledge and the dissemination of established basic knowledge—may be in serious competition with each other, especially if the teaching profession serves as a recruitment pool for IRAD personnel and if IRAD job opportunities attract promising college graduates away from schoolteaching.

Since the production and reproduction of knowledge nowadays is almost completely a government concern, an imbalance cannot be corrected by free enterprise. Schools are maintained chiefly by local government with the help of state government; more than 50 percent of research and development is financed directly by the central government; and a substantial part of industry-financed IRAD is indirectly paid for by the government when it allows the IRAD payrolls to be deducted from the corporations' taxable incomes. Even the part of IRAD that is not paid for by the Government is—according to many authorities—largely dependent on incentives held out by the governmental system of patent protection for inventions. Thus, whatever imbalance develops within the area of the production and reproduction of knowledge, as well as between the production of knowledge and the production of investment goods and consumers' goods, is not to be blamed on the competitive economic order but on the inadequacies of governmental planning.

These are not just academic speculations but very real problems of urgent concern to our democratic process. The high taxes needed to finance education and research cannot but impinge on the production of other things, and industry feels the pinch not a little (as does every taxpayer). On the other hand, the neglect of education is becoming increasingly notorious and is to a large extent attributable to the inflationary increases of wages and salaries in industry, which have made the financial rewards to teachers and scholars inadequate for the maintenance of the required supply.

RATIONAL RESOURCE ALLOCATION

With the pressure of competing demands on the productive resources of the nation that exists today, the problem of allocation of resources deserves more thought than it has been given. According to their special interests, or often out of sheer enthusiasm, different groups try to promote increased outlays for capital investment, increased expenditures for education, increased disbursements for IRAD, and increased consumer spending, all at once—not just in times of depression (when it would make sense) but all the time. Of course, every one of these increases would be fine to have, but since they compete with one another we should first make up our collective minds regarding the comparative advantages. No matter whether an increase in industrial research is financed by the Government or by private industry (under the patent system or with some other stimulus), the decision to increase inventive activities is fully rational only when it seems likely that productivity can be raised faster and maintained more securely through more new technical knowledge than through more capital equipment, more basic research, or more education. If the total amount of productive resources that can be withheld from the production of consumers' goods is limited (as it must be), how much should be allocated to the production of capital goods, how much to the reproduction of established knowledge, how much to the acquisition of new basic knowledge, and how much to the production of increased technical knowledge? This is a matter for economic judgment, tempered by important political and moral considerations. It would surely be foolish to allot to IRAD *all* the resources that can be spared from the consumption sector; it would be stupid to allot *none* of the available resources to IRAD. Even very far within these extremes there may be too much promotion or too little promotion of IRAD.

It has become fashionable among students of economic growth and development to acclaim technological progress as the number-one factor in the process. This may be perfectly justified, but it does not imply that IRAD should be singled out as the most important of all pursuits. Some of those who stress IRAD in order to reduce the emphasis upon capital investment forget that the increase in the stock of capital goods may have been a necessary condition of all technological development. Others who play up IRAD at the expense of liberal education and of basic research forget the dependence of technological research upon advances in basic knowledge and upon an adequate supply of highly educated people. If one puts education, training, research, and development all into one category and sets it against investment in industrial plant and equipment, then one might possibly find evidence for the contention that—in some countries and over some periods of time—the investment in knowledge has contributed more per dollar to the increase in labor productivity than the investment in physical industrial facilities. The bracketing of research with education is necessary for this statement to be tenable; for, among other things, the researchers and developers must have been previously educated and trained, and the utilization of new technical knowledge often requires degrees of dissemination and comprehension that cannot be attained without broad and general education.

If it should be possible to find statistical criteria for the identification of the specific contributions which "investment in knowledge" and investment in physical facilities have made to the increase in productivity, and thereby to obtain evidence for claiming "major credit" for the former, one would have to guard against the mistakes of regarding these findings as pertinent for other places, other times, and other allocations of resources. Particularly one would have to guard against the fallacy of confusing "total utility" and "average utility" with "incremental (marginal) utility." It is perfectly possible for technological research to deserve first prize in the distribution of merits for economic growth and, nevertheless, not to deserve first claim on additional resources.

Lest these remarks be understood as an attack on IRAD, or as a plea for drastic curtailments of IRAD expenditures, be it noted that such has not been my intention. I have intended to show that there *can* be too much IRAD work, not that there *has* been too much of it. Whether the present rate of IRAD expenditures is too high, too low, or just right, I do not know—though I am impressed with the present plight of education and cannot help looking askance at any so clearly identified rival bidder for potential teachers. In any case, a warning is in order against the position of the IRAD enthusiasts who champion the idea of "the more the better."

Policies for Economic Growth

THE COUNCIL OF ECONOMIC ADVISERS

The Council of Economic Advisers consults with the President on matters of economic policy before the executive branch of the Federal Government. At the time this statement was prepared its members were Walter W. Heller, chairman, Kermit Gordon, and James Tobin. In this essay, which appeared in its Annual Report for 1962, the Council discusses the contribution that national policy measures can make to economic growth.

THE GROWTH of the U.S. economy results primarily from decisions taken by individuals, families, and firms. However, all levels of government—Federal, State and local—have a role in the promotion of economic growth. It is no part of that role to force on unwilling households and business firms any particular rate of growth in their own individual activities. But if, as a Nation, we desire a higher rate of growth, there are two consequences for government policy. First, in those areas of economic activity traditionally allotted to some level of government, public expenditures must provide services which contribute to the growth of potential output and which satisfy the needs that accompany increasing income and wealth. Second, public policy—notably in the fields of taxation, education, training, welfare, and the control of money and credit—inevitably stimulates or retards the growth potential of the private economy, even if no such result is consciously intended. Accelerated economic growth requires coordinated policy at all levels of government to facilitate the increase of productivity and the expansion of capacity. . . .

Economic growth is the product of growth in the labor force and growth in productivity. Productivity is preserved and increased primarily through acts of investment: investment in the improvement of human resources, in the creation of new technical and managerial knowledge, in the development of natural resources, and in the formation of physical capital. In the case of investment in human capital and in research and development, the link between expenditure and yield is difficult to measure, but there can be little doubt that the return is substantial. In regard to investment in plant and equipment and the development of natural resources, there is more statistical evidence available. No one of these investments can make its full contribution to the objective of accelerated growth without the others. Each of them is necessary; there is good reason to believe that together they can be sufficient, if vigorously pursued.

INVESTMENT IN HUMAN RESOURCES

Americans have long spoken of foregoing consumption today in order to invest in their children's education and thus in a better tomorrow. For an economy, just as for an individual, the use of the word *invest* in this connection is clearly justified, since it is precisely the sacrifice of consumption in the present to make possible a more abundant future that constitutes the common characteristic of all forms of investment. That devoting resources to education and health is, in part, an act of investment in human capital explains why programs in the area of education and health are economic growth programs. This kind of investment has a long and remarkable history. Rough estimates, which take into account differences in the length of the school year and in school attendance, suggest that the stock of equivalent school years in the labor force rose more than sixfold between 1900 and 1957. The annual rate of growth of the stock of education was more than 3 percent, or about twice the rate of growth of the labor force itself.

Failure to pursue vigorous educational and health policies and programs leads to smaller increases in output in the long run; it is also associated with higher expenditures in the short run. If we fail to invest sufficiently in medical research, we lose not only what stricken individuals might have produced had they been well, but also the use of the resources and funds currently devoted to their care. Failure to invest sufficiently in education means that we will lose the additional output that would be possible with a better educated labor force; it may also mean the perpetuation of social problems necessitating public expenditures. Recognition of the costs of inadequate investment in social welfare is one of the reasons for the Administration's concern to strengthen family services in the public welfare field.

It is a waste of resources to restrict health and education to those who can afford them. Moreover, in addition to each person's interest in his own health and education, there is a public interest in everybody's health and education. The well-being of each citizen contributes to the well-being of others. As a result, we have organized programs to help the population to obtain a quality education, to require attendance in schools, to help ourselves and others to obtain needed medical care, to require that certain medical precautions, such as vaccinations, be taken by everyone.

Education · Estimates made by private scholars suggest that about one-half of the growth in output in the United States in the last 50 years has resulted from factors other than increases in physical capital and man-hours worked. Education is one of the "other factors." Even without allowance for the impact of education on invention and innovation, its contribution appears to account for between one-fourth and one-half of that part of the increase of output between 1929 and 1956 not accounted for by the increased inputs of capital and labor. Education is of vital importance in preparing the skilled labor force demanded by new investment and new technology.

Education's contribution to output is reflected by the well-documented fact that income—a measure of each individual's contribution to production—tends to rise with educational attainment. Of course, not all differences in money income are the result of education. Differences in native ability as well as parental economic and social status are also reflected. Nevertheless, a substantial proportion of the increase in income at increasing levels of education may be attributed to that education.

In 1930, $3.2 billion (3.3 percent of GNP in current prices) was spent for all schools at all levels of education. In 1960, expenditures had risen to about $24.6 billion (5.0 percent of GNP). In turn, in 1930, 29.0 percent of the population 17 years old graduated from high school. By 1958 this was true for 64.8 percent. Similarly, in higher education the number of earned degrees conferred rose from 140,000 in 1930 to 490,000 in 1960.

Though significant progress has been made, substantial opportunities and needs for investment in education still exist. There is a pressing need to improve curricula and teaching methods, make education more readily available to students of merit by reduction of financial barriers, expand facilities and staff to meet rising enrollments, improve the quality and productivity of our teaching staffs and increase their salaries, and narrow the gap in opportunities available to students in different parts of our country. These problems must be met—and met quickly—at all levels of government and at all levels of education if our standards of education are to keep abreast of our needs.

Health · U.S. economic growth in the twentieth century has been associated with better health of the population as a whole as well as an increase in per capita expenditures on health and medical care. Public and private expenditures on health care increased from $3.6 billion, or 3.5 percent of GNP, in 1929 to $26.5 billion, or 5.4 percent of GNP, in 1960. This has been accompanied by a sharp increase in life expectancy and a reduction in death rates from communicable diseases.

At the same time that economic growth has contributed to an improvement in the health of our people, better health has contributed to economic growth. Better health makes possible an increase in the size of the labor force and in the effectiveness of effort on the job.

Further improvements in health would yield significant economic, as well as human, benefits. On an average day in 1960, 1.3 million employed persons—2 percent of civilian employment— were absent from work because of illness or accident. The days of work lost because of illness far exceeded the days of work lost because of industrial disputes; in fiscal year 1960, "currently employed" persons lost a total of 371 million days from work as a result of illness or injury, while the loss from industrial disputes in 1960 totaled 19 million days.

Public support for medical research, the most basic of investments in better health, has been growing. In fiscal year 1962, total expenditures will exceed a billion dollars, of which 60 percent is supported by the Federal Government. Further expansion of research activities, where funds can be wisely spent and where qualified research personnel exist, is desirable both for humanitarian and economic reasons. Much of the necessary research is carried on by doctors of medicine. More rapid expansion of the number of physicians is required to insure that patient care needs, teaching needs, and research needs can all be met. This will be true even if needed improvements are made in the organization and financing of medical care. The Administration has presented a program to authorize Federal grants for the construction of medical, dental, osteopathic, and public health teaching facilities, project grants to plan for new facilities and improved educational programs, and scholarship aid to students.

Eliminating Racial Discrimination · Although significant reductions in discriminatory barriers have been accomplished in recent years, important problems remain. Many nonwhite families are trapped in a vicious circle: Job discrimination and lack of education limit their employment opportunities and result in low and unstable incomes; low incomes, combined with direct discriminations, reduce attainable levels of health and skill and thus limit occupational choice and income in the future; limited job opportunities result in limited availability of vocational education and apprenticeship training. Unless action is taken, today's training practices, affecting tomorrow's employment possibilities, will help to perpetuate inequitable employment patterns.

Our economy loses when individuals who are capable of acquiring skills are denied opportunities for training and are forced into the ranks of the unskilled, and when individuals with education, skill, and training face discriminatory hiring practices that result in their employment in low productivity jobs.

Discrimination is reflected in the distribution of income and in disparities in the levels of education attained by white and nonwhite groups. Nonwhite families had a median money income of $3,233 in 1960. Although this represents a remarkable advance over the figure of $2,099 for 1947 (in 1960 prices), the magnitude of the problem still remaining is indicated by the fact that in 1960 the median income for white families was $5,835.

In 1947, 11 percent of the nonwhite population 14 years of age and over was illiterate; by 1959, this percentage had dropped to 7.5, with declines registered in every age group. The figure was, however, considerably higher than the 1.6 percent illiterate in the white population.

In December 1961 nonwhite workers made up less than 12 percent of the labor force, but accounted for 22 percent of the total unemployed and 24 percent of those unemployed 15 weeks or more.

Economic growth will be furthered by the adoption of nondiscriminatory policies and practices to insure that all Americans may develop their abilities to the fullest extent and that these abilities will be used. The Department of Justice, the President's Committee on Equal Employment Opportunities, and the U.S. Commission on Civil Rights are already acting vigorously. They should be joined in the campaign by all parts of our population and all units of government, business, and labor.

INVESTMENT IN TECHNOLOGICAL PROGRESS

Technological knowledge sets limits on the productivity of labor and capital. As the frontiers of technology are pushed ahead, industrial practice and productivity follow, sometimes pressing close on the best that is known, sometimes lagging behind, with the gap varying from industry to industry and from firm to firm. A stimulus to economic growth can come either from increasing the rate at which the frontiers are advancing or from bringing the technology actually in use closer to the frontiers.

Research and Development · The advance of technological knowledge depends on the amount and effectiveness of the human and material resources devoted to research and development. The limited data available suggest that within industries and between industries there is a positive correlation between research effort and productivity growth. However, some of the most important developments affecting the productivity of a firm or industry may originate from research done by equipment and material suppliers, or from basic research done by government and the universities. The benefits of research activity are often widely shared.

Expenditures on research and development in 1960 totaled about $14 billion. In 1961 the total was probably in the neighborhood of $15 billion, nearly three times the expenditures in 1953, and almost a third as large as business expenditures on fixed capital. Between 1953 and 1960, research and development as a percentage of GNP in current prices doubled from 1.4 percent to 2.8 percent.

Research and development cover a wide range of activities aimed at increasing the stock of scientific and technical knowledge. As we move from basic research to applied research and to development, the goals become more closely defined in terms of specific practical objectives, the predictability of the results increases, and the benefits become less diffuse. More than 90 percent of research and development spending is for applied research and development—most of it for development. Slightly less than 10 percent is for basic research.

Approximately three-fourths of the Nation's total research and development effort is performed by industry, and over half of this is financed by the Federal Government. Profit considerations naturally lead private firms to concentrate on developing and improving marketable products. Even here, supplementary government support can pay off handsomely. Estimates suggest that hybrid corn research, of which perhaps one-third was publicly supported, yielded a substantial return to society over and above the returns to farmers and seed producers.

Less than one-third of all basic research is done by industry. Government, the universities, and other nonprofit institutions, although doing only one-fourth of total research, do most of the Nation's basic research. Such research seldom results directly or immediately in new products and processes. But in the long run, basic research is the key to important advances in technology. Fundamental inventions like the transistor—an outgrowth of basic research in solid-state physics—may revolutionize large sectors of industry and have a tremendous ultimate effect on productivity.

The Federal Government plays a much larger role in financing than in performing research. It is estimated that in 1961 the Government paid for about two-thirds of the total national research effort including, in addition to work done in government laboratories, almost 60 percent of the research undertaken in industry-run laboratories and over 70 percent of the research done by universities. About 70 percent of government research and development spending is accounted for by the Department of Defense. The Atomic Energy Commission and National Aeronautics and Space Administration together account for nearly 20 percent.

In addition to its direct contributions to research and development spending, the Federal Government has stimulated private research and development activity. The science information services of the National Science Foundation, the Atomic Energy Commission, the Office of Technical Services of the Department of Commerce, and other government agencies contribute to the over-all efficiency of national research and development. Federal tax law encourages research and development by making such costs fully deductible in the year they are incurred. The Small Business Act encourages spending on research and development, including cooperative research, by small companies. Moreover, the Federal Government makes an important contribution to the training of future research scientists and engineers through its support of education and basic research in the universities.

STRENGTHENING RESEARCH AND DEVELOPMENT. During the 1950's, the number of professional scientists and engineers in the United States increased at an annual rate of approximately 6 percent. Total resources allocated to research and development grew at an even faster rate because a rising proportion of all scientists and engineers were engaged in research, and because supporting personnel, equipment, and material per research scientist increased. During the 1960's, these trends will continue, but one limit to growth will be the supply of scientists and engineers in certain fields. Future investment in research will be limited largely by the quantity and quality of earlier investment in education.

Overemphasis on current research and development activity should not be permitted to erode the underlying educational base. Just as research is investment for the economy, education is investment for research. The needs for educational expansion stressed earlier in this chapter include urgent requirements for laboratories, laboratory equipment, and other science teaching facilities.

A greater share of research and development resources and talent should be devoted to basic research and prototype development and experimentation in fields which promise major advances in civilian technology. Military research helped to create such important discoveries as isotope medicine, the computer, and the jet engine. The important impact on civilian technology of these offspring of military research suggests that high returns might be achieved if sights were set higher in nonmilitary research. Since the risks of basic research and experimental development are very great, and since the rewards for success are not confined to single firms or even industries, there is a case for public support to attract additional resources into this work.

In a number of industries, firms which are highly efficient in production and marketing may be too small to undertake an efficient research and development program. In others, a research tradition is lacking, or research is discouraged because the benefits tend to diffuse beyond the market grasp of individual firms. In agriculture, all these conditions are present, and the high returns to society from government support of research suggest that comparable programs to increase research in certain manufacturing industries might be highly desirable.

More Effective Use of Existing Technology · (1) In some industries there are legal obstacles to technical change. The housing construction codes of many localities provide a prominent example. In principle, these codes protect the public from shoddy construction; in practice, they often prevent the use of new materials, designs, and techniques which are superior to the old, and a lack of uniformity among codes in different localities discourages mass production of certain prefabricated housing components. With respect to construction codes in particular, the Housing and Home Finance Agency should continue to encourage the adoption of performance standards for codes and should strengthen its programs of testing and evaluation.

(2) American labor has a remarkable record of acceptance of new technology; but understandable resistance to the displacement of labor by new equipment has occasionally developed when opportunities for retraining and re-employment were not clearly visible. The Federal Government can help considerably, first, by pursuing effective policies to maintain full employment, and second, by expanding and improving its programs in job training and retraining.

(3) The process of technological change would be smoother if society knew better how to reap the rewards and reduce the costs. Research in the social, behavioral, and managerial sciences can lead to more efficient use of resources and to quicker grasp of the opportunities afforded by technological progress.

(4) Innovation is facilitated by a flow of information about new technical developments. Since many firms, especially small ones, are not in a position to follow new technological developments closely, the Government can play a useful role by providing business with relevant information and analysis.

(5) The Panel on Civilian Technology, composed of a group of distinguished scientists, engineers, businessmen, and economists, has been brought together under the joint auspices of the office of the President's Special Assistant for Science and Technology, the Department of Commerce, and the Council of Eco-

nomic Advisers. The panel is examining opportunities for stimulating civilian research and development as well as for more effective use of existing technology. It has begun to address itself
particularly to those sectors of our economy where major social
and economic benefits could be expected to accrue from technological advances.

(6) By eliminating monopolistic and collusive barriers to the
entry of new business and by maintaining the spur of competition
to innovation and the utilization of technology, antitrust enforce-
ment tends to create conditions which encourage economic
growth.

INVESTMENT IN PLANT AND EQUIPMENT

Between the resourcefulness of the labor force and the ideas of
the laboratory on one side and the satisfaction of consumption
needs on the other, the indissoluble link is the economy's stock
of plant and machinery. Our own history and the experience of
other industrial countries alike demonstrate the connection between physical investment and growth of productive capacity.
Without investment in new and renewed plant and equipment,
skills and inventions remain preconditions of growth; with it,
they become ingredients.

Investment as a Source of Growth · Investment in fixed capital
leads to increased capacity both by equipping new members
of the labor force with capital up to existing standards and by
providing greater amounts for all workers. Since 1929, the stock
of privately owned plant and equipment (in constant prices) has
grown relative to private man-hours worked by nearly 80 percent
and by nearly 50 percent relative to the private labor force.
Nearly all of the latter increase has taken place during the post-
war period. Between 1929 and 1947, the rate of investment was
sufficient only to provide enough capital—although more modern
capital—to keep pace with a growing labor supply. No increase
in capital per worker occurred. Since 1947, the rate of growth in
the ratio of capital stock to labor supply has been approximately
2.7 percent a year, but there is a perceptible difference between
the growth records of the first and second halves of the postwar
period. From 1947 to 1954, the amount of capital per worker increased by 3.5 percent a year; in contrast, the annual increase

from 1954 to 1960 averaged only 1.9 percent.

The importance of investment in the growth process is suggested by the parallel movement of the growth of potential output per man and the growth of capital per man (Table 1). Both

Table 1.—Growth in Business Potential Capital-labor and
Output-labor Ratios, 1929–60

[Percent per year]

Item	1929 to 1947	1947 to 1960	1947 to 1954	1954 to 1960
Capital stock per worker [1]	0.0	2.7	3.5	1.9
Output per worker [2]	1.5	2.8	3.3	2.1

1. Business capital stock is built up from private purchases of plant and equipment, with allowance for retirements; excludes religious, educational, hospital, other institutional, and farm residential construction.

2. Business output is gross national product minus product originating in general government, government enterprises, households and institutions, the rest of the world, and services of existing houses.

SOURCE: Council of Economic Advisers.

ratios grew more rapidly after 1947 than before, and more rapidly between 1947 and 1954 than subsequently. In general, the experience since 1929 supports the belief that the more rapidly the capital stock grows relative to the labor force, the greater will be the growth in potential output per worker, provided that other necessary conditions are met.

Though there was no increase in capital per worker between 1929 and 1947, there was a slow increase in productivity which must be attributed to technical progress and to improvement in the quality of both labor and capital. When, as in subsequent years, investment was more rapid, there was an accompanying acceleration of productivity gains. These gains were not simply the result of the separate contributions of the advance of knowledge, the improved skills of the working population, and the rise in capital per worker, but came in large part from the interaction of all three.

Investment in new equipment serves as a vehicle for technological improvements and is perhaps the most important way in which laboratory discoveries become incorporated in the production process. Without their embodiment in new equipment, many new ideas would lie fallow. Conversely, the impact of a dollar's investment on the quality of the capital stock depends on how rapidly increases in knowledge have taken place. This interaction between investment and technological change permits each worker to have not only more tools, but better tools as well.

The slower rate of growth of the capital stock in recent years provides one explanation for the accompanying slower growth of labor productivity and potential output. The proportion of output devoted to investment, and the rate of growth of the capital stock itself, are measures of the diversion of current resources to the creation of future capacity. During the period 1947–54, expenditures on business fixed investment averaged 11.0 percent of GNP and the stock grew at an annual rate of 4.2 percent (valued in 1961 prices). In the period 1955–60, 9.8 percent of GNP was invested and the capital stock grew at an annual rate of 3.2 percent. The ratio of investment to potential GNP is even more relevant; in this case, the ratios are 10.9 percent and 9.4 percent for the two periods. This difference of 1.5 percent in the fraction of potential GNP invested represents nearly $45 billion of additional capital.

Policies to Encourage Investment · (1) ADEQUATE LEVELS OF DEMAND. The single most important stimulant to investment is the maintenance of full utilization of capacity. The historical record shows that when output falls below its potential the rate of growth of the capital stock declines. Expected profit from investment is strongly influenced by the expected demand for the output that the new capital will help produce, even if the investment is meant largely for cost reduction rather than capacity expansion. Estimates of future demand are colored by the experience of the present and the recent past. During periods of economic slack, estimates of future demand are relatively pessimistic, and many projects are foregone which would appear profitable under conditions of high demand.

There is a tendency to think of profitable investment opportunities for the whole economy as exhaustible: the more of them that are used up in any one year, the fewer remain. There may be some validity to this view for a single industry, which can mistakenly expand its capacity beyond the possibilities of future market demand. But for the entire economy, what appears as unavoidable excess capacity is in fact avoidable deficiency of demand. There are, and always will be, unsatisfied wants for a higher standard of living, though the demand for any particular product may perhaps be satiated.

It is true that, with any given level of technology, a higher rate of investment can occur only through the acceptance of investment opportunities of lower profitability. But appropriate tax and monetary measures can make even these investments sufficiently attractive. And technical progress can have the same effect. To equip a more rapidly growing labor force also demands a larger volume of investment relative to potential GNP. Fortunately, if actual output is held close to a rising potential output, faster labor force growth will open opportunities for additions to plant and equipment which would be economically unattractive if the labor supply situation were tighter. Thus a higher ratio of investment to output can be more easily maintained. When excess capacity already exists, however, profitability is low for that reason alone, and the growing labor force appears as a threat, instead of the stimulus to investment it really is.

In addition to serving as an indicator of future profits, the level of aggregate demand, through its impact on current profits, plays an important role in providing finance for investment. A policy that sustains near-capacity operations goes beyond strengthening the profitability of investment; it insures an ample supply of low-cost internal funds, which itself encourages investment.

(2) MONETARY AND CREDIT POLICY. The open market operations of the Federal Reserve and the debt-management operations of the Treasury exert a powerful influence on supply conditions in credit markets. If economic growth were the only end to be served, the sole object of monetary and credit policy would be to assure an adequate flow of funds to finance the needed capital formation at interest rates appropriate to the basic profitability of investment.

Use of monetary techniques for growth purposes must, of course, be limited by the demands placed on them by other national objectives. In the present situation, for example, monetary policy has a role to play in the attainment of recovery from recession and in the restoration of balance of payments equilibrium. Policies for growth and recovery are complementary, since any policy that stimulates investment will simultaneously stimulate aggregate demand. This situation, however, will not always prevail. When excessive demand threatens inflation, stability and growth goals will tend to push monetary policy in opposite directions. At such times, the importance of economic growth would suggest the major use of other measures—principally budgetary surpluses—to achieve stability. For when demand is strong enough to generate pressure on existing capacity, and only then, rapid growth requires that enough resources be withheld from other uses to make a sustained high rate of investment possible without inflation. Under these circumstances, a surplus in the Federal budget plays the constructive role of adding to national saving and making resources available for investment. The role of a policy of monetary ease at full employment is then to insure that the resources freed by a tight fiscal policy are indeed used for investment and not wasted in unemployment.

The current balance of payments problem puts additional constraints on the use of monetary policy to promote recovery and growth. If low interest rates encourage foreign borrowing in the U.S. and a large outflow of funds seeking higher yields abroad, monetary policy may have to be more restrictive than domestic objectives alone would dictate. We need monetary techniques that can serve both masters at once. But difficult decisions of balance between conflicting objectives may sometimes be unavoidable.

(3) TAX POLICY. Every tax system is the product of particular needs and economic conditions; no tax system can be neutral in its effects on the ways in which households and business firms earn and spend their incomes. If faster economic growth is desired, revision of the tax structure is called for, to permit a higher rate of investment once full use of resources is achieved.

The Administration's program encompasses two complementary approaches to this objective. The first is an investment tax credit equal to 8 percent of investment in eligible machinery and equipment; the second is revision of the guidelines for the tax lives of properties subject to depreciation.

The investment credit will stimulate investment by reducing the net cost of acquiring depreciable assets, thus increasing expected profitability. The increase will vary inversely with the expected life of the asset. For an asset with a service life of 10 years and an after-tax yield of 10 percent before the credit, the investment credit will increase the expected rate of return by about one-third. The increase in net yield will be greater for less durable equipment and smaller for more durable equipment.

Investment decisions are also influenced by the availability of funds. The investment tax credit will increase by some $1.5 billion the flow of cash available for investment under conditions anticipated for 1962.

Since the credit applies only to newly acquired assets, the entire incentive effect is concentrated on the profitability of new capital and no revenue is lost in raising the profitability of assets already held by business firms. It is an efficient way of encouraging re-equipment and modernization of productive facilities, as well as the expansion of capacity. The credit will thus help to accelerate economic growth and improve our competitive position. It will also increase the attractiveness of investment at home relative to direct investment abroad. In both ways the credit will help to ease our balance of payments problem.

Revision of tax lives for depreciable property is desirable as a matter of equity to reflect more accurately the influence of obsolescence on economic lives of capital assets. Present guidelines were established 20 years ago on the basis of replacement practices of the depressed prewar years. Depreciation, designed to reflect the loss in value of plant and equipment over time, is a function not alone of "wear and tear," but also of technological progress, changes in the relative costs of economic inputs, competitive conditions, and consumer tastes and demand. Through its favorable effects on cash flows, expected rates of return, and risk, liberalized depreciation will tend to stimulate investment.

Attention to Federal income tax adjustments to stimulate investment must not be allowed to obscure the role of State and local tax policies and practices in economic growth. The tax collections of these governments are nearly half as large as Federal collections.

The power to tax under this governmental system is shared by thousands of separate jurisdictions. Improved coordination among them will improve economic efficiency. Identical tax sources are frequently utilized by two, three, and even four layers of government without appropriate cooperation. Taxing authorities occasionally use their powers in ways that capriciously affect decisions concerning the location of plants and disrupt normal competition. The result may be a misallocation of resources and economic loss.

The Congress has recognized the need for better intergovernmental coordination. It has provided for the creation of the Advisory Commission on Intergovernmental Relations to foster "the fullest cooperation and coordination of activities between the levels of government." The Advisory Commission, composed of representatives of the executive and legislative branches of all levels of government, has already made important recommendations for the coordination of local taxes by the States and for improved tax coordination and cooperation between Federal and State governments.

INVESTMENT IN NATURAL RESOURCES

Economic growth is not simply a matter of growth in the size and skills of the labor force, in the quantity and quality of capital goods, and in the productivity of the processes by which these inputs are combined. It is equally a matter of turning more and more of the earth's endowment of natural wealth—soil, sunlight, air, water, minerals, plant and animal life—to the purposes of man. America's position has generally been one of natural plenty, but we cannot complacently assume that the abundance of the past will also characterize the future.

But neither is there any reason to suppose that resource limitations will in the foreseeable future place serious limits on the growth of the economy. Technological change, substitution of abundant and cheap raw materials for scarce and expensive ones, investment in improved resource management and conservation, and increased reliance on imports all provide important offsets to the effects of increasing scarcity on the real cost of obtaining resource inputs. Taken together, these factors tend to keep the economy growing along the path of least resistance so far as its resource requirements are concerned. If the various offsets to increasing scarcity are not fully effective, resources can be obtained by digging and drilling deeper, utilizing lower grade deposits, constructing dams and better waste treatment facilities, and other measures involving higher costs. But the necessity to devote more labor and capital to these tasks would constitute a drag on the economy, tending to cancel some of the efforts we make to stimulate growth.

The Historical Record · A rough judgment as to the probable consequences of continued depletion of resources in the future can be derived by examining the record of the past. The long-term trend of raw materials prices relative to the prices of finished products is a useful, though by no means ideal, indicator of the effectiveness of the offsets to natural scarcity.

From 1900–04 to 1955–57—the last period for which data are available—the over-all index of raw-materials prices increased by 25½ percent, an average rate of increase just over 0.4 percent per year. The most striking feature of the record, however, is not this slow but visible trend toward increasing costs as our resource endowment has been exploited more intensively but the varying patterns of price movement shown by different commodities and by the same commodity at different times.

The lessons to be drawn from such past trends are these: First, it is likely that increasing resource scarcity has had only a negligible retarding effect on economic growth during the present century. Rising real costs of obtaining some resources have been largely compensated by declining costs of obtaining others. Second, the historical record does not indicate that more rapid economic growth will simply result in our "running out of resources" more quickly. On the contrary, past investments have permitted resources to be extracted more efficiently and used more efficiently.

Public policy has contributed to this success by limitation of economic waste, the development and adoption of improved methods in agriculture, forestry, and other fields, the unified development of river valleys, and a variety of other measures. Finally, the opportunity to obtain raw materials from abroad has been important in the past and will be increasingly important in the future.

Water Resources · There is wide agreement that one of the most serious resource problems facing the United States at present and in the immediate future is the development of water resources. The use of water has been increasing rapidly as a result of population growth, higher living standards, increasing urbanization, rapid growth of industries that are heavy users of water, increases in the amount of land under irrigation, and other factors. In the Eastern United States and the Pacific Northwest, the problem presented by these trends can be met for the next few decades by an adequate and appropriately timed program of investment in (1) multiple purpose water resource development which, in addition to other benefits, permits the collection and storage of water for use as needed and (2) facilities for treatment of industrial and municipal wastes. In some of the dry regions of the West, however, the opportunities for further development of water resources will be exhausted within the next two decades. Barring major scientific breakthroughs, the continued economic development of these regions will soon come to depend upon how effectively an almost fixed supply of water is used to satisfy the most important of the various industrial, agricultural, and municipal needs for water.

It is certain that additional investment to increase the quantity and to improve the quality of the supplies of water will be a major part of any solution to the problem. Pollution control, in particular, will require major investment expenditures in the coming decades. Additional research and development in methods of conserving and augmenting water supplies, including desalinization, weather modification, reduction of evaporation losses, cheaper and more effective waste treatment and more efficient use of water in industry and agriculture may produce high returns.

Since expensive investments must be undertaken to increase the quantity and quality of water supplies, it is appropriate that the costs be reflected in prices charged industrial and agricultural users. The burdens of scarcity on the economy cannot be entirely eliminated by using scarce capital to augment the supply of scarce water. But the burden can be minimized by a proper balance between investments in increased supply on the one hand, and price increases to eliminate inefficient use on the other.

Agricultural Land · The problem of agricultural land stands in sharp contrast to the problem of water resources. Whereas in the latter the problems requiring attention are those posed by increasing scarcity, in the former they are problems of adjusting to abundance.

The Department of Agriculture currently has plans for a long-range land use adjustment program. This program has three major facets: transfer of cropland to grass; transfer of cropland to forest; and greater emphasis on wildlife and recreational development in the small watershed programs. As the program develops, it will be possible for supply management to place less emphasis on temporary diversion of acreage from the production of specific crops.

The present problems of U.S. agriculture, which reflect in part the fact that the pace of technological progress in agriculture exceeds the rate of growth in demand for farm products, should not blind us to the important lessons to be drawn from the record. When strong policy measures are taken well in advance, technological progress affords an escape from increasing scarcity. Indeed, it is technology that largely determines which portions of the environment are regarded as resources and which are not. Research not only makes possible the more effective use of existing resources, as in the case of agriculture, but may create important new ones. The record of agriculture also illustrates, however, the long lag between the decision to act and the appearance of the benefits. Careful and continuing analysis of present and future resource needs, coupled with readiness to act when the indications of potential difficulties become persuasive, is the best hope for success in meeting the resource requirements of rapid economic growth.

INVESTMENT IN PUBLIC SERVICES

Accelerated economic growth will require increased public investment, just as it will require increased private investment. Without additional plant and equipment, governments at all levels will be unable to meet the increased demands for public services that arise both as a consequence of measures taken to stimulate growth and as a consequence of growth itself. If a high and rising educational level of the labor force is sought as a means to speed economic growth, additional investment in school and college buildings, furnishings, and laboratory equipment will be required. Demands for transportation of both people and goods will increase as a result of economic growth; meeting these demands will require additional investment in urban public transportation systems, airports, roads and highways.

Failure to make adequate investments in the physical basis of public services inevitably retards economic growth. In some cases, the connection is fairly easy to trace; inadequate investment in highways will bring an increase in congestion, with consequent declines in the productivity of trucks and truck drivers, and rising transportation costs. In other cases, the process by which a shortage of basic public services tends to retard the growth of output is less obvious, but no less real; education is an important example. As has been noted above, an inadequate effort to solve the water pollution problem will be paid for in higher costs of obtaining water of adequate quality—unless it is paid for by a decline in the health of the population and decreased productivity in water-using industrial processes. Inadequacy of public services also has effects on economic welfare that are not reflected in aggregate economic statistics. Commuters are well aware of the sacrifice of time that results from inadequate urban transportation systems. The sacrifice of recreational opportunities resulting from failure to make sufficient provisions for public parks as cities expand is another example.

The task of meeting the transportation, recreation, education, housing, and other needs of growing metropolitan areas poses a major challenge to our existing forms of political organization at the State and local level. Public facilities serving the needs of individual political jurisdictions within an urban area are often less efficient than they would be if they had been designed for all, or a large part, of the area. For example, lack of effective and well coordinated land use planning and zoning regulation has resulted in locational patterns of residential, commercial, and industrial developments that intensify transportation problems. Improved planning and coordination can increase the efficiency of public services and make cities better places in which to live. Progress can be achieved through continued Federal assistance to States and local bodies for the planning of urban area development, comprehensive urban renewal programs within cities, public improvement programs, and specific public improvements.

Although the Federal Government is making an important contribution to the solution of problems whose significance extends beyond the boundaries of political units at lower levels, it must be remembered that civil government is basically a State and local responsibility.

INVESTMENT IN HOUSING

The higher standard of living made possible by economic growth results from increased output of a wide variety of goods and services. Among these is one item which, by virtue of its economic importance, its great influence on the general quality of life, and the unique character of the capital investment required to expand its supply, deserves special attention in a discussion of economic growth. This item is housing.

The value of the current services supplied by the Nation's residential structures—the total of rents paid plus the imputed rental value of owner-occupied dwellings—accounted for 13.1 percent of personal consumption expenditures in 1961, or 8.5 percent of GNP. Another 4.1 percent of GNP was accounted for by residential nonfarm construction—the total expenditures on replacing, improving, and adding to the nonfarm portion of the stock of residential structures. That stock itself represents roughly one-fourth of our national wealth, about twice the share accounted for by producers' durable equipment.

These figures are, in part, a statistical image of the importance of the basic human need for shelter. To a greater extent, however, they reflect the fact that better housing is among the most important benefits that economic progress can confer. A dwelling that provides adequate protection against the elements may nevertheless be a serious hazard to the mental and physical health of its occupants, if it is overcrowded, lacking in hot and cold running water or plumbing facilities, or structurally unsound. A better home provides a healthier, safer, and more comfortable living environment; it affords greater opportunities for recreation, aesthetic enjoyment, and peace and quiet.

Few, if any, Americans actually lack a roof over their heads. But about one-fifth of the Nation's housing units are classified as "dilapidated" or else lack one or more of the basic plumbing facilities. Like the poverty that it reflects, substandard housing is a burden borne to a disproportionate extent by a few groups in the society; the aged, the nonwhite, the poorly educated, and families without a male breadwinner. The burden is perhaps most regrettable when it renders ineffective the measures society takes to promote equality of opportunity. The child who has no decent place in which to study can hardly take full advantage of the free education that is provided to him.

A sharp rise in the rate of household formation will occur in the latter part of this decade, reflecting the high birth rates of the middle and late 1940's. It is all the more important, therefore, that substantial progress in improving the average quality of the

Nation's housing be made in the early part of the decade, when the need to increase its quantity will be less urgent. The enactment in the last session of Congress of the Administration-sponsored Housing Act of 1961 was a major step toward meeting the Nation's housing needs. In addition to extending and expanding existing programs for public housing, housing for the elderly, college housing, and farm housing, the Act provides for major new programs of FHA-insured loans to finance construction and rehabilitation of housing for moderate income families, and long-term FHA-insured home repair loans. These new types of loans are eligible for purchase by FNMA. Other important provisions make Federal assistance available to States and localities for various measures in the field of urban affairs, including planning, loans, and demonstration grants for mass transportation projects, and acquisition of land for permanent open-space uses, such as parks. Additional funds were authorized to finance the construction of community facilities. Finally, a series of provisions make additional assistance available for households and businesses displaced by urban renewal programs or other government actions.

The concern here has been the source of rising productive potential and the policies that can strengthen them. Granted continued prosperity, we can have slower growth or faster growth. There is substitution between the composition of output in the present and the level of output in the future. Just as a single individual can increase his consumption possibilities in the future by present saving, so can a whole society provide more fully for its future by using present resources for acts of investment in the broadest sense. No absolute reduction in current consumption need occur; it is only necessary that consumption grow less rapidly than total output for a time. Indeed, future levels of consumption will be higher than they could otherwise be—the cost is primarily in postponement. Happily, for an advanced society like ours, much of what is described from this point of view as investment can also be seen as present enjoyment of some of the delights of civilization: widespread education, good health, and the search for knowledge.

Suggested Further Readings

Abramovitz, M., *Resource and Output Trends in the United States since 1870* (Occasional Paper No. 52, National Bureau of Economic Research, 1956).

Bergson, A., *The Real National Income of Soviet Russia since 1928* (Harvard, 1961).

Bronfenbrenner, M., "The High Cost of Economic Development," *Land Economics,* May and August 1953.

Campbell, R. W., *Soviet Economic Power* (Houghton Mifflin, 1960, paper).

Chamber of Commerce, *The Promise of Economic Growth: Prospects, Costs, Conditions* (1960, paper).

Clark, C., *Growthmanship: A Study of the Mythology of Investment* (Hutchins, 1961, paper).

Committee for Economic Development, *The Budget and Economic Growth* (1959, paper).

Deane, P., "The Long Term Trends in World Economic Growth," *Malayan Economic Review,* October 1961.

de Grazia, S., *Of Time, Work and Leisure* (Twentieth Century Fund, 1962).

Denison, E. F., *The Sources of Economic Growth in the United States* (Committee for Economic Development, 1962, paper).

Domar, E. D., *Essays in the Theory of Economic Growth* (Oxford, New York, 1957).

Eckstein, O., "Federal Expenditure Policy for Economic Growth," *The Journal of Finance,* May 1962.

Fellner, W. J., "Rapid Growth as an Objective of Economic Policy," *Annual Proceedings of the American Economic Association,* May 1960.

————, *Trends and Cycles in Economic Activity* (Henry Holt, 1956).

Galbraith, J. K., *The Affluent Society* (Houghton Mifflin, 1958).

Griliches, Z., "Research Costs and Social Returns: Hybrid Corn and Related Innovations," *Journal of Political Economy,* October 1958.

Hall, C. H., *Fiscal Policy for Stable Growth* (Holt, Rinehart and Winston, 1960).

Harrod, R. F., *Towards a Dynamic Economics* (Macmillan, London, 1948).

International Economic Association, *The Theory of Capital,* D. C. Hague, ed. (Macmillan, 1961).

Jacobsen, H. B. and J. S. Roucek, eds., *Automation and Society* (Philosophical Library, 1962).

Knorr, K. and W. Baumol, *What Price Economic Growth?* (Prentice-Hall, 1961, paper).

Knowles, J., *The Potential Economic Growth of the United States,* Study Paper No. 20, Joint Economic Committee, U.S. Congress (Government Printing Office, 1960, paper).

Kuznets, S., *Capital in the American Economy* (Princeton, 1962).

———, *Six Lectures on Economic Growth* (Free Press, 1960).

Lewis, W. A., *The Theory of Economic Growth* (Irwin, 1955).

Massell, B. F., "A Disaggregated View of Technical Change," *Journal of Political Economy,* December 1961.

Meade, J. E., *A Neoclassical Theory of Economic Growth* (Oxford, New York, 1961).

National Bureau of Economic Research, *The Rate and Direction of Inventive Activity,* R. R. Nelson, ed. (Princeton, 1962).

Nelson, R. R., "The Simple Economics of Basic Scientific Research," *Journal of Political Economy,* June 1959.

Phelps, E. S., "The Golden Rule of Accumulation," *American Economic Review,* September 1961.

———, "The New View of Investment," *Quarterly Journal of Economics,* November 1962.

Pitchford, J. D., "Growth and the Elasticity of Factor Substitution," *Economic Record,* December 1960.

Ramsey, F. P., "A Mathematical Theory of Saving," *Economic Journal,* September 1928.

Rockefeller Brothers Fund, *The Challenge to America: Its Economic and Social Aspects* (Doubleday, 1958, paper).

Rostow, W. W., *The Process of Economic Growth,* 2nd edn. (Norton, 1962, paper).

———, *The Stages of Economic Growth* (Cambridge, 1960, paper).

Schultz, T. W., "Education and Economic Growth," *Social Forces Influencing American Education* (National Society for the Study of Education, 1961).

Silk, L. S., *The Research Revolution* (McGraw-Hill, 1961).

Slichter, S., *Economic Growth in the United States* (Louisiana State, 1961).

Solow, R. M., "Investment and Technical Progress," *Mathematical Methods in the Social Sciences* (Stanford, 1960).

———, "Technological Change and the Aggregate Production Function," *Review of Economics and Statistics,* August 1957.

———, "Technical Progress, Capital Formation and Economic Growth," *Annual Proceedings* of the American Economic Association, May 1962.

Spulber, N., *The Soviet Economy* (Norton, 1962).

Swan, T., "Economic Growth and Capital Accumulation," *Economic Record,* November 1956.

"A Symposium on Capital and Economic Growth," *Review of Economic Studies,* June 1962.

Tobin, J., "A Dynamic Aggregative Model," *Journal of Political Economy,* April 1955.

Ture, N. B., "Growth Aspects of Federal Tax Policy," *The Journal of Finance,* May 1962.

United States Congress, *Employment, Growth and Price Levels,* Joint Economic Committee (Government Printing Office, 1959, 1960).

Young, A., "Increasing Returns and Economic Progress," *Economic Journal,* December 1928.